This Book must be returned on or before the date marked below

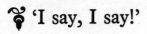 'I say, I say!'

'I say, I say!'

*Great Britain's Best Corny Jokes and
the Debatable Wit and Wisdom of*

MICHAEL WATTS

SIDGWICK & JACKSON
LONDON

First published 1971

Copyright © Sidgwick and Jackson Limited

ISBN 0 283 97806 6

Printed in Great Britain by
The Anchor Press Ltd, and bound by
Wm. Brendon & Son Ltd, both of Tiptree, Essex
for
Sidgwick & Jackson Limited
1 Tavistock Chambers, Bloomsbury Way, London WC1

For Matthew, Charles,
Joanna Louise and Simon

Contents

[Illustrations by WILLIAM MARTIN]

Introduction

Ladies and Gentlemen . . .

This book contains the best of British Corn. Not all the best, to be sure. But a rich harvest, nevertheless. A veritable Cornucopia.

It is unlikely that every joke will be new to you. Equally, it is unlikely that you will have heard all of them before. (And if you have, you will be hearing them again, won't you?)

It is unlikely that every joke will give you a chuckle. Equally, it is unlikely that all of them will fail. (And if they do, don't blame me. I am not personally responsible.)

In addition to this splendid collection of Corny Jokes you will find some random ramblings for which I do claim responsibility. While I recognize that my experiences are exceedingly limited, and may well be of exceedingly limited interest . . . (VOICE FROM THE BACK OF THE HALL: 'Then why write a ruddy book about them?' CHAIRMAN: 'Order! Let the man speak.') . . . it is my earnest hope that into your drab lives . . . ('Sauce! Who the devil does he think he's talking to?') . . . they may bring a little sunshine. ('Good grief! He gets worse and worse.') Far be it from me, however, to suggest that . . . ('Oh, take him off!'—'Bo-oo!'—'Get on with it!')

CHAIRMAN: 'Order! Er, Mr Watts. I have no doubt that we are all most eager to hear what you have to say. But we do not, I am sure, want to take up too much of your valuable time. So perhaps if you would, ah—get on with it. . . .'

The Corny Joke Philosophy

The Simple Soul will laugh at corny jokes
But groans come from Sophisticated folks.
The More-Sophisticated fall about—
They know what corny jokes are all about.

Anon.

Were I to be told that I must be deprived of all my senses (I know —some would say I have taken leave of them already) I would fight for my sense of humour.

It is one of the most precious qualities a human being* can possess. At the same time it is unknown (unknown to me, anyway) for any human being to admit that he does not possess it. Men may confess—it has been said—to treason, murder, arson, or wearing a wig, but they will not own up to a lack of humour.

Happily I can enter a plea of 'Not Guilty' on all counts—on the first four as a matter of fact, and on the last, even more fervently, as a matter of honest opinion.

To opine, 'The trouble with you is that you haven't got a sense of humour' is to invite the angry retort, 'This fist says I *have*!' In which case you would be well advised to back down, and agree with the fist. So let us take the easy way out, and assume that we

---

* My apologies for describing you as a Human Being, which is a clumsy expression. 'Being' presumably means existing, and is therefore superfluous. (It is sufficient, for instance, to describe a pig as a Pig. There is no need to call it a Pig Being. A pig which has never existed cannot be described. A pig which used to exist could be called a Dead Pig or, possibly an Ex- or Former Pig. But an existing pig is a Pig.) This does not alter the fact that, on its own, the category Human has a disagreeable science fiction ring about it. To add Being somehow makes Human sound more 'human', if you see what I mean.

all have a sense of humour. But that your sense of humour may differ from mine.

If everybody is satisfied with that, we can get to the nub—Corn.

Look again at Anon's couplets at the head of this chapter. He quite rightly implies that some humans, The Groaners, have a very low opinion of Corn. Oh, they will hotly deny that they lack a Sense of Humour. But Corn, they think, is beneath them. The Groaners are supported by my dictionary, which defines corny, in the context of jokes, as 'out of date, old-fashioned'. And corny jokes *are* old-fashioned—in the sense that they were first fashioned many years ago. Here's one:

A mosquito lands on the ear of an elephant and whispers: 'Mind if I snatch a ride?'

'Not at all,' says the elephant. 'I didn't notice you landing, and I shan't notice you taking off.'

Hardly a side-splitter, I agree. But before you give it the thumbs-down, I should explain that this was discovered on a Babylonian tablet of the 7th century B.C. Nine hundred years later it still had them chortling in Rome. And it might even raise a faint smile today.

The fact that it is probably the most feeble corny joke you have ever heard (the Best is Yet to Come!) proves my point. It is not a patch on today's Corn—precisely because over the centuries Corny Jokesters have been beavering away improving their material to ensure that, like all living traditions, it moves with the times.

So the dictionary is wrong. Corny doesn't mean 'old-fashioned'. 'Traditional' is the word. Humour itself is traditional. Therefore humour is corny. Therefore the best humour must be Corn with a capital C. *Q.E.D.*

We first taste Corn at a tender age—usually in the form of riddle-puns. Your average nipper does not need to be in the world for very long before he can appreciate: Q: 'When is a door not a door?' A: 'When it's ajar.'

We all heard that one pretty early in life. And had great success in telling it—thanks to indulgent grown-ups who affected to be

2

unaware of the condition under which a door was not a door.

But the first *proper* corny joke I can recall hearing is:

'I say, I say—grand day for the race.'

'What race?'

'The human race.'

Tickled pink with that, I was. Thought it was fantastically clever stuff. And when I trotted it out to my contemporaries they all roared with laughter. For there are no Groaners among little children. The Sophisticated bit comes later, with adolescence.

In my case, the Groaning phase passed quickly, when I found that the veneer of sophistication prevented me from enjoying Corn to the full. So I progressed to that higher 'More-Sophisticated' plane (as praised by Anon).

The Groaner will maintain that I have merely slipped back again into childhood, and that I delight in Corn because I am one of Anon's 'Simple Souls'. He's welcome to his opinion, poor fish. But pity him—he doesn't know what he's missing.

Not included in this book are bales of specialized Corn—such as the **'Knock-knock'** jokes. Sample:

(Knock, knock) Who's there?—Amos. Amos who?—A mosquito.

(Knock, knock) Who's there?—Anna. Anna who?—Another mosquito.

(Knock, knock) Who's there?—Wurzel. Wurzel who?—Wurzel these mosquitoes coming from?

Neat. But the knock-knock specialists and their ilk must agree that they comprise only a small part of the whole.

Nor will you find here more recent categories of jokes which may eventually mature into Corn, but have yet to serve their time. Such as:

Elephant Jokes

'How can you tell if an elephant has been in the fridge?'—'Look for his footprints in the butter.'

or:

3

'How do you get four elephants in a mini-car?'—'Two in the front and two in the back.'

Crossing Jokes (as popularized by Master David Frost)
'What do you get if you cross a zebra with a whale?'—'A traffic jam.'
'What do you get if you cross a pig with a billy-goat?'—'A crashing boar.'

Contemporary Riddles
'What lies shivering on the bottom of the sea?'—'A nervous wreck.'
Two catch riddles I do rather like are: 'What is green and has four wheels?—Grass. I lied about the wheels.'
and:
'What has four legs and barks?'—'A dog.'—'Curses! You've already heard it.'

Sick Jokes are out for ever, as far as I am concerned. They are a travesty of Corn, and—here comes the pun—go right against the grain.

What you *will* find in this book is a broadly based selection of Great British Corny Jokes—many of prime vintage, aged in the wood for decades.
You will discern certain peculiarities. Waiters, for example, are very much more popular subjects than, say, milkmen. (I suppose there is only one basic joke about the milkman—he does his best to encourage it!) Dogs are infinitely more popular than cats. And men are infinitely more popular than women—in so far as they tend to be the winners, while the ladies tend to be the losers. (Not always, but the tendency is very marked.)
For the record, here is the corny joke which I have found to be Britain's most popular—though not the best, by a long chalk:
'I say, I say! Where are you off to in such a hurry?'

'I'm going to the doctor—don't like the look of my wife.'
'Hang on, I'll come with you—I hate the sight of mine.'
—*Oi!*

See what I mean about the women coming off worst? That joke would be just as good, or as bad, if the word 'wife' were changed to 'husband'. But it never is. Perhaps husbands wouldn't get it.

I say 🎗 a mixed bag

To put you in the mood, here is a corny gallimaufry (you may have to look that up) for a curtain raiser.

🎗 *'I say, I say! Which skins make the best slippers?*
'I don't know. Which skins make the best slippers?'
'Banana skins.'
—Oi!

🎗 'What's the difference between a buffalo and a bison?'
'You can't wash your hands in a buffalo.'

🎗 *'I say, I swallowed a pillow this morning.'*
'Really? How do you feel now?'
'Oh, a little down in the mouth.'

🎗 'Wish I had enough cash to buy St Paul's Cathedral.'
'Why on earth do you want to buy St Paul's Cathedral?'
'I don't. Just wish I had the cash.'

Native returns from a hard day's hunting with a disappointing 'bag'—a pygmy and a snake. But his wife is delighted:
🎗 *'Splendid! Now we can have snake and pygmy pie.'*

🎗 'I say. Do you believe in clubs for women?'
'Yes—but try kindness first.'

Two goats scavenging on a rubbish tip. One finds a roll of old film, and chews it up.

6

'Did you enjoy the film?'
'Not really. I preferred the book.'

'I say—I bought a silk dress while I was in India. It cost £100.'
'Sari?'
'No. I'm delighted with it.'

'What did your uncle leave in his will?'
'Only an old clock.'
'Won't be much bother winding up his estate.'

'I say, that woman looks like Helen Green.'
'You should see her in red.'

'I say, can you lend me a fiver for a week, old man?'
'Depends which weak old man it's for.'

'How did you find the weather on holiday?'
'Just went outside the hotel, and there it was.'

After years of wedded bliss the husband breaks the bad news—
he's already married to someone else.
'I think that's pretty small of you,' says his wife.
'Really? I thought it was bigamy.'

'Did you have any trouble in the floods?'
'I'll say. Had to float out of the bedroom window on my double-bass.'
'What about the wife?'
'Oh, she accompanied me on the piano.'
—Oi!

LOCKED OUT

Had you been in Chelsea around that midnight hour, you might have observed me scampering barefoot through the streets in my pyjamas. ('Extraordinary behaviour! There's a rum feller-me-lad, if you like. Must be bombed out of his mind. Silly young idiot!')

Yes, indeed. I would sympathize with all these outraged exclamations. Quite, quite reasonable from your point of view. And had I been in your shoes I would, without doubt, have joined your disapproving chorus. But had *you* been in *my* shoes—or, rather, without them—I think that you too would have adopted my apparently extreme course of action.

The fault was partly mine, and partly that of the Americans.

As I say, it was coming up to midnight and time for bed. I had performed my normal closing-down routine, and the only remaining chore was to put the plastic dustbin in the corridor outside the door of my bachelor flat.

Now, this door is self-closing, a convenience which I have always found slightly inconvenient. One *can* slip the latch, but I regard that as chicken—and I rather enjoy living dangerously. In the course of time I had developed a nifty manœuvre in which I

9

took great pride: 1. Open the door. 2. Pick up the dustbin (both hands needed). 3. Rumba the hip so that the door swings wide. 4. Pop the dustbin down and slip back inside before the door completes its return journey.

There's efficiency for you.

On this particular occasion, however, I was handicapped. Tucked under one arm I had my portable radio, to catch the Moonshot latest on Midnight Newsroom. That's what did for me. It was All Systems Go for seven-eighths of the Nifty Manœuvre. But before I could return to base—clunk!—the door beat me to it.

The radio, the dustbin, and me. So unfair. Just one second later and I would have been home and dry. Why, oh why, had I fixed those blessed screws to stop burglars slipping the latch? Then, if only I were married—a little tap on the door and I would be rescued in a jiffy.

No use dreaming, though. Let us apply the brain to reality. There *must* be a way.

Knock up the neighbours? Not a good idea at midnight—and anyway that still wouldn't get me back into the flat. Break down the door? No axe. And the racket would not make me too popular either. Break a window, then, and clamber in? No go. Although I live on the ground floor, there is a basement-well surrounded by spiked railings. And I didn't relish negotiating those in the dark, especially in bare feet.

Call the police? Well, they refer you to the fire-brigade, who break a window and charge you a few quid into the bargain. And how could I telephone them? One does not, as a rule, carry small change in one's pyjamas. But there must be a way. There must be.

Then it came to me that some time ago, with uncharacteristic foresight, I had bought a spare key for the flat, and had left it in a drawer at the office. Eureka? Not quite. For (curses!) I couldn't drive to the office—no car keys. So what would you do, chum? Only one thing for it. Find a taxi.

When you are locked out at midnight in your pyjamas, no dressing-gown and no slippers, you feel pathetically alone and strangely vulnerable. Although it was a mild night I decided that the sooner I could be tucked up in bed the better, so I set off hot-foot for the King's Road. (Hot, by the way, is the word—make no mistake about that. Those of you who have tried sprinting barefoot over tarmac will wince at their recollection of such crass foolhardiness.)

But it's a strange thing. Leaping about the streets at night in your pyjamas is really quite elating. You feel you are achieving something which is beyond the experience of ordinary mortals. Also that you might, in one way or another, be breaking the law. A sort of cross between Superman and Jack the Ripper.

This exhilarating sensation, however, quickly evaporated. And so did my enthusiasm for sprinting. By the time I arrived at the King's Road I had slowed, limping, to the pace of a snail. (Not a limping snail, you understand. I could manage a little better than that. But progress was sluggish.)

Despite the lateness of the hour, the King's Road was still pretty busy. (You know what a wild bunch those Chelsea types are. With the exception of myself, they never sleep.) And there were too many folk about for comfort. One became the object of great interest. Purposefully, I avoided meeting their gaze. Rather like the bashful nipper who covers his eyes with his hands and pretends you can't see him.

On the other hand, the object of the exercise was to collar a cab. And when one is trying to attract the attention of cabbies, one does not play the shrinking violet. I spotted a taxi, leapt out into the road, and hailed it. The driver failed to stop. He saw me all right, the blighter! But he obviously didn't want to involve himself in anything unsavoury. Along came another. Same reaction.

One shouldn't blame them really, I suppose. Pyjamas provide perfectly adequate cover—although they would probably cause a few raised eyebrows in the Savoy Grill—but they do not inspire confidence in others. At last a cabby took pity on me. I explained the predicament—and the understanding fellow took it all in his stride and ferried me to the office.

The Night Watch at work gave me a rougher ride. I had to run a gauntlet of badinage before I was allowed to get at that key.

'There's nothing worse,' I concluded as I nursed the burning soles of the old feet in the cab back to Chelsea, 'than being locked out at midnight in your pyjamas.'

It has since crossed my mind that there is one thing worse. But *that* doesn't bear thinking about.

I say ❦ in the bosom of the family

Traditionally, it is mother-in-law who comes in for most stick from comedians. Whether or not you consider her a fair target will presumably depend on your experience of mothers-in-law. But if you *are* a mother-in-law you will regard this constant pillorying as grossly unjust—especially as fathers-in-law go scot free.

Aunts, too, seem to get more than their fair share of ridicule. Again the male escapes. For uncles are rarely objects of derision. And when it comes to wedded blistering, it is usually the wife who gets battered. She is seldom allowed to better her lord-and-master.

Almost invariably, the male fires the ammo. The female is his target, his Aunt Sally. (Note to Women's Liberationists: Picket those country fairgrounds: 'Aunt Sallies—Out! Out! Out! Uncle Sidneys—In! In! In!')

I am content with the *status quo* (Natch). It is obvious where my sympathies lie. I suppose it to be a spin-off from the eternal sex war. But, paradoxically, when the ladies have the chance to hit back they don't seem to take it. True, comediennes have always been pretty thin on the ground. Yet those that *are* in business seem to direct most of their fire at their own sex. A clear indication that they have no chance of winning the battle of the sexes. No chance.

The preceding apologia will, I hope, justify the largely anti-feminine bias in the following material. Sorry, girls, it's the way of the world. . . .

❦ *'I say, I say! I've just lost 180 lb. of ugly fat.'*
'How did you manage that?'

'*I divorced her.*'
—Oi!
(*Yes, I know. I've* really *burned my boats with that one. Still, start as you mean to go on, I always say.*)

Husband sneaking home at 2 a.m. is met on the stairs by his wife, brandishing a rolling pin. She's *furious.*
 'SO! Home *is* the best place after all, eh?'
'I don't know about that—but it's the only place open.'

 '*I say, I say! I always take my wife morning tea in my pyjamas.*'
'*Very thoughtful.*'
'*Yes—but my pyjamas are getting a bit soggy.*'

 'My wife has sinus trouble.'
'Sinus trouble? I'm sorry.'
'Yes. It's—sign us a cheque for this, sign us a cheque for that. . . .'

Small boy during tea:
 '*Father, are caterpillars good to eat?*'
'*Don't talk about that sort of thing at the table. We'll discuss it later.*'
And later:
'*Now what was that about caterpillars?*'
'*Oh, never mind. There was a fat one on your salad. But it's gone now.*'

 'I say, we're having Great Aunt Miranda for lunch on Christmas Day.'
'Marvellous. She can't possibly be tougher than last year's turkey.'

 '*Our dog bit my mother-in-law this morning. So I've just taken him to the vet.*'

'To have him destroyed?'
'No—to get his teeth sharpened.'

'I say, Dad! There's a man at the front door with a moustache.'
'Tell him I've already got one.'

'I say, I say! My wife drives me to drink.'
'You're lucky. I have to walk all the way.'

Chap telephones his wife to say he is bringing the boss home for dinner. But he arrives home alone.

'Where,' asks his wife, all dressed up for the occasion, 'is the boss?'
'Sorry, I lied, dear. It's just that I felt like a decent dinner for a change.'

'Daddy, can you help me with this crossword? I can't solve the final clue.'
'Ask your mother. She always has the last word.'

'I say. I've just got a bottle of whisky for my mother-in-law.'
'Sounds like a bargain.'

'Do you know how to make your own anti-freeze?'
'Fill her hot water bottle with ice.'

Chap catches his wife with the milkman:

'How long has this been going on?'
'Since we installed central heating.'
'What's that got to do with it?'
'It used to be the coalman.'

Wife opens the door to her husband:

'What do you mean by coming home half drunk at this time of night?'
'Sorry, my darling. I ran out of money.'

'For twenty-five years my wife and I were ideally happy.'
'Then what happened?'
'We met.'
—*Oi!*

THE MAGIC
INFURIATING FORMULA

How do you best go about infuriating a fellow? I know it sounds rather an odd question to ask. For why should one want to infuriate a fellow? You will no doubt protest that you wouldn't dream of nettling anyone deliberately.

But hold hard.

Can you honestly claim that you have never, in all your puff, found yourself in a situation where an adversary has the upper hand and the only way to triumph is to make him lose his cool?

No, I bet you can't claim that. And even if you are so brimful of goodwill to all men that you prefer peace at any price, you may still benefit from the little story that follows. You can regard it as a cautionary tale. . . .

I stumbled on the Magic Infuriating Formula quite by accident. It was the best of crisp and sunny mornings, and driving to the office I was feeling well disposed to all my fellows. A day when the last thing one bargains for is trouble at t'mill, one might say.

Rounding the bend, I came upon the usual fairy-lit shanty town of huts, machinery and improvised barriers which indicates to the sharp motorist that there are Men At Work on the road. This particular thoroughfare is always being dug up for one reason or another, and then resurfaced. It is a continuous operation rather like painting the Forth Bridge. Once the job is completed, they start all over again at the beginning. The show never closes, and it keeps Us, and Them, amused.

Anyway, I found that the lads were concentrating their activities that morning on the very spot at which I daily made a right turn across the crown of the road into a side street. It did not appear to present too much of a problem, for the lads had obligingly (as I thought then) left a gap between their excavations, through which traffic could pass.

I was about half-way across when the roadman hailed me: 'What the dickens do you think you're doing?'

To be absolutely accurate, I should qualify this quotation. He did not say 'What the dickens?' (An expression which has nothing to do with Charles, by the way. Dickens is supposed to refer to the devil, but how the dickens it originated I just don't know.) He employed a more forceful word which, in deference to propriety, I have expurgated. But the chap's meaning was clear enough. He wanted to know what I was doing.

I explained I was turning a corner, no less.

18

'You can't go across here, mate.'

'Why not?'

'It's not ready.'

'In that case,' I replied chirpily, 'why don't you fence it off, Sunny Jim?'

Until that moment, the fellow had been your average roadman-in-the-street. A bit free with the dickenses, perhaps, but off duty quite probably an extremely congenial cove. A worthy member of the human race. Now his human qualities were abandoned. My words had turned him into a raging beast.

'Wodja mean calling me Sunny Jim?'

'Well, I ... Nothing, really, I ...'

'Don't you call ME Sunny Jim, mate!'

He thrust a flushed and fiery face through the car window—which I had opened at the start of the conversation—and snarled. Then the f. and f.f. was withdrawn (dislodging the cap that had rested above it) and reinforcements were summoned.

Soon there were about half a dozen owners of f. and f.fs. leaping about and snarling around the car. I felt just like that chap in the red E-type which stalls in a wolf-packed forest because, silly man, he isn't using the petrol with the Mileage Ingredient. Fortunately, though, I still had enough fuel for my getaway. So I beat it. Leaving—as I observed through the rear-view mirror—a forest of furiously shaking fists.

Now the point about all this is that I hadn't *meant* to be patronizing or anything. The words Sunny Jim were intended not to enrage, but to humour. Yet they had the opposite effect to that desired. And the effect was lasting.

After parking the car, my route to the office took me back down the side street and past the roadmen's shanty town again. One of the lads spotted me.

'There he is! There he is!'

They moved, as one man, towards me. Well, I'm sure, almost sure, that it wouldn't have come to blows. Not if I had anything to do with it, anyway. I am one of nature's peace-at-any-pricers —mainly because I know well who would come off worst in any physical wrangle. And it wouldn't be half a dozen roadmen. A cheery grin didn't seem to pacify them, so I withdrew once more into the side street, and took a roundabout route to work that day. Also the next day. And the next. For each time I neared the shanty town I would be sighted by one of its inhabitants, who would set them all baying.

A whole week passed before operations had progressed far enough along the road for me to make a safe crossing.

Since my encounter with the roadmen, I have experimented further with the Magic Infuriating Formula, using Sunny Jim during mild altercations where I felt there was a danger of being worsted.

Always it has the same devastating effect of throwing folk into varying degrees of ferment. My adventure with the Shanty Town Lads was like a vicar's tea party (sorry about that, Vicar) compared with some of my more recent experiments. It is a complete mystery. But I promise you that these two apparently cheery and inoffensive words are absolute dynamite.

You try them and see.

I say 🎯 at work

The butt of Corny Jokes at work is, more often than not, the boss. It would be rash, however, for an up-and-coming young chap to blight a bright future. So I am playing safe and restricting such jibes to the minimum.

🎯 Boss: *'You should have been here at nine o'clock.'*
'Why, what happened?'
—Oi!

Foreman to weedy young applicant for tree-felling job:
🎯 'Where on earth did *you* learn to chop down trees?'
'In the Sahara.'
'But there are no trees in the Sahara.'
'Not now, sir. Not now.'

🎯 *'Excuse me, sir. The Invisible Man's outside.'*
'Tell him I can't see him.'

Old gent in the back of a Rolls-Royce which has crashed into a ditch:
🎯 'By gad, James, you're fired! You nearly killed me.'
'Oh sir, give me another chance.'

At the lunch break two workers open up their sandwiches.
🎯 *'Blimey, cheese again. It's cheese, cheese, cheese. I'm fed up with ruddy cheese every day.'*
'Why don't you ask the wife to make something else?'
'No good—I'm not married. I make my own.'

'You're twenty minutes late again! Don't you know what time we start work at this office?'
'No, sir. You're always hard at it when I arrive.'

 'Hello. Is that Hall, Hall and Hall Ltd?'
'No. This is Hall, Ltd.'
'Oh—wrong number. Sorry you've been trebled.'

 'Come along now,' bawls the foreman. 'I want that rotten fruit picked up. And you—I want that stinking fish moved. Jump to it!'
'I know what *he* wants,' mutters one of the lads.
'Oh yes? And what do I want, eh?'
'You want that rotten fruit picked up, and . . .'

 'I say! That's an expensive fur coat for a struggling young typist like you.'
'Yes—but I stopped struggling.'

Chap is waltzing with the managing director's wife at the firm's dinner-dance.
 'Gracious!' puffs the boss's good lady. 'I'm danced out.'
'Oh, I wouldn't say that,' says her partner. 'Just pleasantly plump.'

 'I say, I say! I'll have to get a potato clock.'
'A potato clock? Why?'
'I'll have to get a potato clock so that I can be at work at nine o'clock.'
—Oi!

THE BRONZER

If you were a man—better still if you *are*, then the question becomes even more pertinent—would you wear make-up? I have little doubt that, be you male or female, you will take a strong line on the subject. And I also have little doubt what the majority view would be.

It is a view you may have to reconsider.

Starting with woad, our male ancestors were great ones for prettying themselves up. Then they rightly came to the conclusion that, as Byron—quoting Shakespeare—put it: ' 'Tis very silly, "To gild refinèd gold, or paint the lily." ' So they left it to the ladies.

Now, however, the refinèd gold gilders and lily painters are back in business.

The revival of their fortunes stems mainly from America, where sales of 'men's grooming aids' bring in umpteen million dollars each year. Over there, many husbands are reputed to spend more time in the bathroom these days than their womenfolk—slapping on skin cream and lotions, hair pieces and toupees (for the bald chest as well as the bald pate) and false eyelashes and powder. The lot.

Lawyers, stockbrokers, politicians—even one or two policemen, apparently—are taking advantage of cosmetic surgery to lose their 'facial sag', bags under the eyes, cauliflower ears (that must be the policemen and politicians) and Durante noses.

Until recently, their British counterparts were content to rub along—and rub in—a spot of Brylcreem and, perhaps, a dash of aftershave. But there are now clear signs that they, too, are lending an ear to the persuasive male lily painters.

How, I hear you sigh, are the mighty fallen! But do not despair. All is not lost. Yet.

Steaming through a London store, I chanced, in the department known there as Men's Toiletries, upon the Bronzer.

Now, the Bronzer is not to be confused with that tan-without-the-sun lotion which has been around for years. I never sampled that myself for, in the early days, its application seemed fraught with problems. You rubbed on the colourless liquid and a couple of hours later—bingo! you had a tan. But unless you took the greatest care, you were in for a nasty shock. For the tan could be embarrassingly uneven.

I noticed a particular tendency for folk to go deep orange around the eyebrow regions. And once the tan appeared, you were stuck with it. It was no use trying to wash it off. You had to let it fade away, all in its own good time.

Actually this provided some splendid opportunities for merry japes. When it first came out, I recall that during the closing stages of a rather hectic party we spied a chap flaked out in an armchair. Someone dashed off and returned with a bottle of the tanning fluid, and a certain word—which need not concern us here—was inscribed on the poor fellow's forehead. It stayed there for days. We felt a bit rotten about it afterwards because he couldn't see the joke (or the word, come to that). But if that's the worst thing that happens to him, he'll be a lucky lad, as they say.

Back to the Bronzer—a very different kettle of fish. For it is real make-up for men. The store girl said it had sold well in

24

America, but I was surprised to hear that she was now doing a roaring trade palming it off on British males. Especially as it cost the best part of three quid a tube. She urged me to try it. After all, she said sweetly, if I didn't like it I could always wash it off.

That was when the real significance of the stuff hit me. Once one has applied it one must avoid washing one's face. It brought home to me how rarely most women can wash their faces.

'Go on!' urged the girl again. 'Try it.'

'Well, I don't know. Doesn't seem quite right, somehow. I'm sure it's fine, but it's just the idea of putting stuff on my face. . . .'

'Ooh—that's old-fashioned,' insisted the girl. And she popped the Bronzer into my hand. 'Go on, silly—try it!'

'All right, then. But *not* on my face.'

I squeezed a blob of the brownish cream from the tube, and decided to apply it to my left thumb. Couldn't do much harm there. Then I thanked the girl for her generosity, explaining that I would have to mull the matter over before stumping up cash for a whole tube. She agreed that the necessary outlay might seem considerable, but promised that I would not be disappointed with the result.

Out in the street, I studied the thumb and held it up for comparison with its fellow on my right hand. Yes, it certainly was very nice and brown. I'm not saying that folk were racing up to me and exclaiming: 'My, my—what a beautifully brown thumb you have there!' But the experiment was definitely a success.

So should I buy a tube? In theory, I reasoned, I'm an ideal candidate. I never seem to find time for much of a summer holiday, so the Bronzer would be my only chance of a proper tan. And if that girl is right and it is selling well I wouldn't be alone in wearing it.

But there was no getting away from it. The thing was make-up. No—not for me. You must live your own life, and make your own decisions. But if you can bring yourself to wear that stuff, then you're a better man than I am, Gunga Din.

And a browner man than I am. Browner, possibly, than good old Gunga Din himself.

I say ❦ at the shops

If Corny Jokes are any guide at all, Britain's shopkeepers must be a remarkably witty crowd. They are masters of the pun and the snappy rejoinder. It would seem that the customer has only to cross the threshold to be subjected to a fusillade of waggish word-play and quick-fire badinage.

And in this Nation of Wisecracking Shopkeepers, it is probably the butcher who has the edge on his rivals when it comes to pawky repartee. (I will resist the irresistible pun about pawk butchers. No point in trying to beat them at their own game, is there?)

❦ *'Four nice chops please, butcher. And make them lean.'*
'Certainly, madam. Which way?'
—Oi!

❦ 'Would madam please refrain from leaning on the bacon slicer?—We are getting a little behind with our orders.'

Chap rushes into the ironmonger's:
❦ *'A mousetrap—and hurry, please, I want to catch a bus.'*
'Sorry, sir. We don't stock 'em that big.'

❦ 'Is this meat tender?'
'As tender as a woman's heart, sir.'
'Then give me a pound of sausages.'

❦ *'I'd like a tablet of soap please.'*
'Would you like it scented.'
'No thank you. I'll take it with me now.'

26

'How much do your packets of manilla envelopes run at?'
'They don't run, sir. They're stationery.'

'Look here, butcher. Those sausages had meat in one end and bread in the other.'
'Sorry, madam. But these days it's hard to make both ends meat.'

'I say, I say! Is this aerosol good for mosquitoes?'
'Certainly not—kills 'em stone dead.'

Chap rushes into a fish and chip shop late at night.
'I say—any chips left?'
'Certainly, sir.'
'Serves you right for frying so many.'

'May I try on that suit in the window?'
'Of course, sir. But I'd rather you used our changing room.'

'I've brought back these rashers. They're bad.'
'Impossible, madam. That bacon was cured only last week.'
'Then it must have had a relapse.'

At the newsagent's:
'I say, do you keep the *Sunday Express* for a week back?'
'No, sir. You'll need a porous plaster for that. Try the chemist.'

'I called an hour ago for my birthday cake. But I had to leave it to be altered—you'd spelt my name with a small H instead of a capital H.'
'Ah, yes sir. It's quite ready for you. I'll put it in a box.'
'No, no! Don't bother—I'm going to eat it now.'

'Is that bread fresh?'
'I'll say it's fresh, madam. We've had to put it on the top shelf to keep it away from the tarts.'

Young man takes his fiancée to the jeweller's to choose the ring.

 'Certainly, sir. Eighteen carat?'
'No, it's an apple. Want a bite?'

 'Yes, madam. These are the best apples we've had for years.'
'Then I'd like to see some you've had more recently.'

 'I say—my wife bought a magnificent fur coat at the sales.
She got it for a ridiculous figure.'
'I know—I've seen it.'

Tailor measures a customer for a new coat.

 'Now sir, how would you like a belt in the back?'
'How would you like a kick in the teeth?'

 'I say, are those sausages I see hanging up in the window?'
'No, madam. They're hanging down.'
—Oi!
(You've got to hand it to those butchers. They don't miss a trick.)

28

FASHION—
The Watts Budget Plan
(and a Spot of Advice from Ecclesiasticus for the Ladies)

It has always been my opinion that the Fashion Designer is among those who enjoy the life of Reilly. He has a really cushy number.

He pops on his thinking chapeau, muses for a few minutes (a few hours if he likes to take his time), dashes off half a dozen sketches, and the ladies flock to buy. It matters not how absurd or way out his designs are, the ladies will enthuse and lap them up. And even if they are less than enthusiastic, the ladies will still wear 'em. For they cannot resist the desire to be 'fashionable'.

It is a real puzzler to me why women allow themselves to be herded this way and that by the trend-setting designers. Why Saint-Laurent, Balmain, Courrèges and the rest are accorded the roles of shepherds.

Once in a while you do come across an independent woman who wilfully strays from the flock and makes up her own mind about what she will wear. I salute her. But such Black Sheep are rare. Most meekly obey the shepherds—and their sheepdogs the fashion writers, who scamper about barking at the stragglers.

From where I stand, the whole scene looks pathetic—the more so because these flocks of sheep traipse round and round in circles.

There is precious little new under the fashion sun, and the shepherds plagiarize like mad. You must have seen the headlines after the Sheepdog Trials: *'Forsooth! 'Tis the Tudor Look!'* or *'Vo-dodee-odo! The Twenties roar in with the Flapper Look!'* or *'Float back to the Thirties with that Harlow Look!'* or *'It's All Clear for the Austerity Look of the Forties!'*

Yawn, yawn. In the world of fashion it is, as they say—or the French say, anyway—*Plus ça change, plus c'est la même chose.* You Briteesh, 'ow you say eet? 'Zee more eet changes, zee more it ees zee same sing,' eh?)

But to ensure that their numbers remain cushy, the designers take care never to produce zee same sing you chose last time you kitted yourself out. For you must not be allowed to carry on sporting your old clobber. That would be bad for the Rag Trade. The designers did not, for instance, reintroduce the Flapper Look in the thirties, any more than they will announce the Sixties Look now. They wait until you have dispatched all your old clothes to the jumble sale. Only then will they declare them to be fashionable once more.

Thus the sheep is constantly having to dip into her reserves to make sure that her coat is kept up to date. Call this the Sheep Dip, if you like. (You don't? Too bad.) But if she were a little more intelligent about it, poor lamb, she would need to use the Sheep Dip less often.

No longer do fashions change by the century, the generation or even the decade. We get mini, midi, maxi, hot pants and more —all within the year. The shepherds have their flock racing round at such a lick that were the wiser sheep to mark time for a few months, they would find themselves back in fashion again. The flock would have chased the full circle.

Bear this in mind while I detail the Watts Budget Plan. . . .

First, ladies, let us get down to the nitty gritty. Why do you want to be fashionable? To please other women, or to please men?

'If you put it *that* way,' bleats the sweet little lamb, 'we do it to please men, I suppose.'

Right. Now let's say that you still have your old minis (plus, perhaps, the odd hot pant) and the shepherds suddenly decree that Minis and Hot Pants are Right Out, and Midis and Long Johns are In. Your problem is to find £40 in the Sheep Dip for your new outfit.

STAGE ONE of the Watts Budget Plan is to accept that if you are really sincere in your desire to please men, you will not buy midis or long johns anyway. So you can put £20 of that £40 back into the Sheep Dip. And carry on wearing minis and hot pants.

STAGE TWO of your pleasure-giving exercise is to invest the remaining £20 in an expensive present for the Man of Your Choice. Or, alternatively, just hand him the cash. Either way, I promise you he will be delighted.

So. You have now halved the cost (you still have that £20 in the Sheep Dip, remember) and doubled the pleasure. Simple, isn't it? And don't forget that you will be sitting pretty when minis and hot pants come back into fashion. Even if you need more, they will be bargain buys, for they take only a third—*preferably much less*—of the material required for garments with less male appeal. If they happen to be out of fashion, better still—they will be at sale prices.

Save £££s with the Watts Budget Plan, me gels. You won't regret it. And neither will I!

Now, what about the £20 you gave to the Man of Your Choice?

Well, you may, if you're lucky, get that back too—in kind if not in cash. At all events, the chances are that the M. of your C. will not blue it on clothes for himself.

It is often said that this is the Peacock Age for men. That these days we are just as prone as women to the dictates of fashion designers. Not quite so, I think.

Certainly we make the odd concession here and there. *But only if it suits us.* The rest we can take or leave. If men don't approve a new style—however 'fashionable' it is said to be—we jolly well won't wear it.

Somewhere here is a clue to the basic difference in the attitudes of the sexes to clothes. Women look on them as mere adornment —and their appetite is tempered only by shortage of cash. But men regard them as friends on whom they can rely.

The Book of Ecclesiasticus advises: 'Forsake not an old friend; for the new is not comparable to him.' And Ecclesiasticus is absolutely spot on.

I haven't bought a suit, or a jacket, or a pair of trousers for at least three years. I even have the uppers of my boots patched rather than chuck them away. Typical of these old, reliable chums are my donkey-brown trousers. Although I've had them for donkey's years they are not yet demoted to weekend wear and still give loyal service two or three days a week.

The Old Reliables started off as cream cavalry twills. But when the ingrained wear became too much, I did a Phyllosan job with brown dye and made them young again. We have been through thick and thin together. And when they have become too thin I've had them patched. In fact, there are now patches in the patches. Only when there are patches in the patches in the patches, will I consider putting them out to weekend grass.

It's not a question of economy. It is fair play. You don't, if you're a decent sort, cast your old friends aside if they become unfashionable. You stand by them. And, as we have established, if you stand by them long enough fashion will turn full circle. So that they, once more, can stand by you.

It is an ideology of which Ecclesiasticus would heartily approve.

32

I say 🎯 in town

Corn can thrive only in the country. But Corny Jokes flourish even though the seed may fall on tarmacadammed ground. And talking of falling . . .

Elderly lady tourist peers down from the top of the Post Office Tower in London and asks the guide:
🎯 *'Do people fall off here often?'*
　'No, madam. Only once.'
　—Oi!

Two tramps meet on the Thames Embankment.
🎯 'Saw you outside the Savoy Hotel last night.'
　'Yus—that's where I'm staying.'
　'What, at the Savoy?'
　'No—outside.'

Policeman in the High Street accosts an itinerant musician.
🎯 *'Have you permission to play your banjo in the street?'*
　'Well, actually, no.'
　'In that case, I must ask you to accompany me.'
　'Certainly, officer. What would you like to sing?'

Landlord pays an ominous visit to a tenant in an old block of flats.
🎯 'I've come to tell you that I'm going to raise the rent.'
　'Thank goodness. Because I can't.'

At the Municipal Boating Lake an eager young fellow starts his first day as an attendant.

33

'Come in, Number 91—your time is up.'
'Hang on lad, we haven't got a 91.'
'Sorry, boss. . . . Are you in trouble, Number 16?'

Pretty maid to guest at the Hilton Hotel:
 'What time do you wish to be called, sir?'
'Eight o'clock sharp—with a kiss, my angel.'
'Very good, sir—I'll tell the porter.'

Two man-eating tigers walking round Piccadilly Circus.
 'I thought you told me,' says one, 'that this was a busy place.'

Attendant at Madame Tussaud's addresses a small group of visitors to the Chamber of Horrors:
 'Who is that lady with you?'
'That's my mother-in-law.'
'Well, keep her moving please—we're stock-taking.'

Magistrate addresses a policeman in the witness box.
 'What made you think the accused was intoxicated?'
'Well, sir. He dropped a penny into the pillar box on West-minster Bridge, looked up at Big Ben, and said: "Strewth, I've lost two stone!" '

Elderly lady to street musician:
 'Tell me, do you always play by ear?'
'No, mum. Sometimes I play round the corner.'

Motorist spots a fellow whose car is wrapped round a lamp post in Oxford Street.
 'Have an accident?'
'No thanks—just had one.'

Chap sees a friend walking along the High Street carrying a huge lobster.

34

'I say, are you taking that lobster home for tea?'
'No, he's had his tea—I'm taking him to the pictures.'

Park-keeper gives a sharp dig in the ribs to a chap sleeping on a bench.
'Hey, you! I'm going to close the gates.'
'All right,' says the chap drowsily. 'Don't slam them, will you?'
—Oi!

. . . and country

Now for some prime examples of rustic humour.

 'I say, I say! My dog's a blacksmith.'
'Prove it.'
'Just give him a kick and he'll make a bolt for the door.'
—Oi!

Hiker, crossing a field where a bull is grazing, calls to the farmer.
 'I say, is that bull safe?'
'Well, he be a darn sight safer than what you be.'

Chap strolling along the river bank comes upon another, struggling in the water.
 'How did you come to fall in?'
'I didn't come to fall in,' gasps the flounderer. 'I came to fish.'

 'I say, I say! Why do cows wear bells?'
'Because their horns don't work.'

 Country postman: 'Yes, ma'am. I've had to walk four miles to the farm with this letter.'
'How annoying for you. But why didn't you send it by post?'

Squire spots a fellow creeping through his spinney late one night.
 'I say, where are you going with that torch?'
'I'm going a-courting, Squire.'
'Nonsense, man! I didn't take a torch with me when I went courting.'
'No, I shouldn't think so by the looks o' your missus.'

36

Country bumpkin arrives at the station booking-office and asks for a return ticket.

🎭 'Where to, sir?'
'Where to? Why, back here o' course!'

Chap sees one of the locals wheeling a barrow-load of manure along the lane.

🎭 'What are you going to do with that?'
'Put it on my rhubarb.'
'That's a change. We have custard on ours.'

Walter was caught trespassing on the estate by no less a person than the Duke himself.

🎭 'I didn't realize this land were yours, Your Grace.'
'Certainly it is.'
'How did you come by it, Your Grace?'
'My ancestors fought for it, my man.'
'That so? Well, take your coat off and I'll fight you for it.'

Gamekeeper catches a chap fishing on the estate:

🎭 'Now then, can't fish 'ere.'
Chap considers this for a moment and replies: 'Dashed if I know.'

Patronizing City gent accosts a yokel:

🎭 'How far is it to Sutton Bonington, Jarge?'
'How did ee know my name was Jarge?'
'I guessed it, my good man. I guessed it.'
'Then ee can guess how far 'tis to Sutton Bonington if ee be so darn smart.'

Vicar watches villager staggering home.

🎭 'Drunk again, Ned.'
'Ar, Vicar, so be I.'

37

'*I say, I say! My dog and I go for a tramp in the woods every single day.*'
'*Does the dog enjoy it?*'
'*Yes, but the tramp's getting a bit fed up.*'
—Oi!

TIME, GENTLEMEN, PLEASE

Day after day and night after night, closing-time at the local brings the landlord and his customers into conflict. He and his good lady sigh with relief as they dim the lights and drape the pumps with towels. The show's over, folks— and mine host and hostess are jolly glad that it is.

The Folks, however, are not at all glad. They have been spending their money freely, and playing their part in building up a convivial atmosphere. Then, just when everything in the beer garden is lovely, the arbitrary law of the land pulls the rug from beneath them.

Ever since the licensing laws were introduced during the First World War there has been growing agitation to do away with them. The boom in tourist traffic has done much to encourage it.

When we go Over There, we get used to the idea of being able to get a drink at all hours. And when They come Over Here, they take a dim view of being denied one.

So the pressure builds up to scrap these 'intolerable and archaic' restrictions. And, until recently, I have been a front-rank campaigner for making them a Thing of the Past. I did spare a thought for those wives who believe that their menfolk spend far too much time already 'taking the dog for a walk'. But I was all for the 'We Never Close' signs to go up outside hostelries throughout the land.

Now I have doubts.

First of all, I share the view of a legal periodical which has summarized the situation rather nicely: 'The system of permitted hours is a compromise between our puritan souls and our commercial natures.' Secondly, it occurs to me that to do away with 'permitted hours' entirely would be to do away with that agreeable business of drinking *after* those permitted hours. This is enjoyed by otherwise law-abiding citizens in town and country alike.

You have to know where to go, of course. And you must be accepted as a regular. But once you are welcomed to 'the club' a pleasant slice of the British Way of Life is in store.

The casual customer is usually unaware of the conspiracy. He notes the dimmed lights and draped pumps and assumes that the show is indeed over. There is no reason for him to think otherwise. The form in the urban local is for the landlord to bawl the traditional 'Time, Gentlemen, Please!' and hustle around yapping 'Thank you, please!' and 'Please, thank you!' until the strangers are seen off.

If you are a regular you do your bit by going through the motions of draining your glass, buttoning up your overcoat, and taking your leave with a resigned, putting-the-best-face-on-it, 'Cheerio!' But you stay put.

Once the landlord and his g.l. have checked the curtains for chinks, up go the lights, off come the towels—and 'club members' can enjoy the thrill of an illicit drink. Understanding policemen recognize that this is hardly a Threat To Society and rarely spoil the fun.

At the country pub it can be even more agreeable. After-hours conviviality at one of my favourites proceeds with the (unofficial) blessing of the law. 'Time' is called, but the cosy click, rattle and slap of dominoes continues. The local constable is in the thick of it, buying his round. And you fall foul of him if you turn down his offer of a pint. That pint is all the better for being 'forbidden'. Abolish the licensing laws and it would taste just like any other.

Mark Twain put it perfectly: 'Adam was but human—this explains it all. He did not want the apple for the apple's sake, he wanted it only because it was forbidden.'

I say ♀ at the local

The pub is naturally one of the best places to tell, and hear, corny jokes. The standard gets better and better as the evening wears on.

At least, it *appears* to get better and better. Next day, when you come to retail some of the winners you picked up the night before, you may be disappointed to discover that members of your audience are less than enthusiastic. You may dismiss them as a humourless shower of wet blankets, but you may find yourself wondering why you had fallen about with quite so much hilarity the previous evening.

You need not look far for the answer. The pub is also much favoured as the setting for some splendid corny jokes—a fair proportion of which involve (1) animals miraculously invested with the power of speech, and (2) gentlemen with eccentric habits. In the following collection, the first two are good examples.

A horse trots into the pub and orders a large brandy and ginger ale. The barman serves his equine customer, who knocks back the drink with considerable relish. Then the horse leans across the bar and observes:

♀ '*I suppose you think it strange that a horse should come in here and ask for a large brandy and ginger ale?*'

'*Not at all,*' *says the barman.* '*I like it that way myself.*'

—Oi!

Chap arrives at the 'Cross Keys' with a dollop of jelly in one ear and a dollop of custard in the other. He orders a pint. The barman serves the customer, but cannot resist pointing out:

🐂 'Excuse me, sir, but you have a dollop of jelly in one ear and a dollop of custard in the other.'

'I'm sorry, you'll have to speak up—I'm a trifle deaf.'

Barman at the 'Flying Horse' serves a customer with his first pint of the day, and remarks:

🐂 *'Looks like rain.'*

'Yes. Tastes like it an' all.'

Fellow in a hacking jacket leads his horse up to the bar of the 'King's Head'.

🐂 'A gallon of whisky for my horse.'

'Gallon of whisky it is, sir. And what will you be having yourself?'

'Oh, just a tomato juice for me. I'm driving.'

Woodworm scuttles into the pub and inquires:

🐂 *'Is the bartender here?'*

Chap enters the saloon bar of the 'White House' hostelry, looks about him, walks up the wall, across the ceiling, down the other wall, and finally orders a pint. When he has downed it, he walks up the wall again, across the ceiling—and out.

🐂 A startled customer exclaims to the barmaid: 'Extraordinary fellow!'

'Yes,' she agrees. 'Never says goodnight.'

Two drinking mates roll up at the 'Red Lion'.

🐂 *'Pint of bitter, barman.'*

'Me too. And make sure the glass is clean this time.'

Barman serves them.

'Two pints of bitter, gents. Er, which one asked for the clean glass?'

The Devil burned off his tail—an occupational hazard—and went into a little corner shop for a replacement.

'Sorry,' said the proprietor. 'We've only got bottles of beer.'
'Then what am I to do?'
'You'll have to find an off-licence where they retail spirits.'

Chap streaks into the 'White Swan':

'*Quick—give me a large Scotch before the fight starts.*' *The barman serves him, and it goes down like a flash.*
'*Quick—give me another large Scotch before the fight starts.*'
Straight down again.
'*Quick—give me another large Scotch before the fight starts.*'
'*Just a minute,*' *says the barman.* '*Where's this fight taking place?*'
'*Right here. I've got no money.*'

'I say, I say, landlord! I know a way you could sell a lot more beer.'
'Jolly good. How could I sell a lot more beer?'
'Just fill the glasses properly.'

A bear ambles into the pub, puts a pound note on the counter and asks for a pint. The barman (having a low opinion of the intelligence of bears) pulls him a pint, but keeps the change. As he hands the tankard to the bear he remarks:

'*This is the first time we've had a bear in here.*'
'*Yes. And the last time too—at these fancy prices.*'

Chap orders a pint at 'The Plough', then picks two gherkins from the dish on the bar counter, stuffs one gherkin in each ear, and leaves. Next night, he does the same. And the next. On the fourth night, the landlord apologizes and explains that they only have pickled onions left. But the chap drinks his beer and then stuffs an onion in each ear.

'I hope you don't mind me asking,' says the landlord. 'But why have you stuck those onions in your ears?'

44

'Because you've run out of gherkins.'

Fellow goes for a pint and parks his hat on the bar counter. The landlord's dog leaps up and grabs it.
'Hey, landlord! Your dog has chewed my hat.'
'Serves you right—you shouldn't have left it on the bar.'
'Look here, I don't like your attitude.'
'It wasn't my 'at he chewed.'
—Oi!

THE MAN YOU CAN TRUST

Who can you trust these days? Us pipe smokers, that's who. The dedicated pipemen of Britain are honest chaps on whom you can rely. Sterling fellows to a man (almost).

You may well dismiss this as biased baloney. And perhaps I am laying it on a bit. There could, I suppose, be one or two pipe smokers around who are absolute scallywags. Nevertheless, there is much more than a germ of truth in what I say.

Look at those Saturday newspaper advertisements for Ex-Canadian Air Force Officers' Macintoshes or Genuine Ex-Government Guards-smart Winter-warmth Shirts. The smug, smiling chaps in the little illustrations that go with them always seem to be pipe smokers. Either clenching their briars between the teeth, or gripping them firmly in their rock fists. Even the fellow in his New and Unissued Officer's-style Underpants.

Now why? Why do you think pipes are placed between the teeth and in the fists of these gentlemen? Quite simply because advertisers know that their prospective customers trust a pipeman. *He* won't sell you a pup. *He* won't let you down. When a pipeman vouchsafes 'My New and Unissued Officer's-style Underpants are tops', folk take him at his word.

If those underpants are good enough for a pipeman, they think to themselves, they are good enough for us.

This, at least, is the way the advertiser's mind works. And advertisers are no mugs, or they would be out of business. They can't afford to be stuck with warehouses crammed to the roof with underpants—even though they are brand-new quality garments styled to suit even the most discerning officer. No sir! They want those warehouses emptied—fast. They need the space. They've just purchased a consignment of Ex-W.R.A.C. Bloomers with Double-gusset.

And your advertiser believes that the best way to get the underpants off his hands (that could have been better put, but let it pass) is to picture them on a pipeman. There can be no other explanation than that over the years people have found by experience that pipe smokers are honourable men.

They are Men of Action too. Picture the winning skipper in a tough ocean yacht race. Imagine his bronzed, weatherbeaten face screwed up against the spray and, yes, you do expect to see a pipe jutting proudly like a figurehead from his jaw.

In addition to their integrity and activity, pipe smokers are also Men of Great Wisdom. Clients who poured out their troubles to Mr Holmes will tell you that not only were their secrets safe with him, but his ability to solve the trickiest problem could be relied upon absolutely.

You may say that, as things have turned out, their confidences have been betrayed. But remember, it was that fellow Watson who blew the gaff. I admit he smoked a pipe too (and cigarettes and cigars on occasion) but he could not, I feel, have been a True

48

Pipeman. As is evidenced by his absurd over-reaction to the cosy fug he encountered one evening on returning from his club:

'My first impression as I opened the door was that a fire had broken out, for the room was so filled with smoke that the light of the lamp upon the table was blurred by it,' he records. 'As I entered, however, my fears were set at rest, for it was the acrid fumes of strong, coarse tobacco—which took me by the throat and set me coughing. Through the haze I had a vision of Holmes in his dressing-gown, coiled up in an arm-chair with his black clay pipe between his lips.'

But the protesting Watson gets his comeuppance in a snappy exchange with the cool pipe-smoking Holmes:

' "Caught cold, Watson?" said he.

"No, it's this poisonous atmosphere."

"I suppose it is pretty thick, now that you mention it."

"Thick! It is intolerable."

"Open the window, then!" ' '

Attaboy, Holmes!

It is unfortunately the case that most folk would side with Dr Watson. The community at large owes much to the British pipemen. But (apart from those pant-pedlars) it fails to appreciate its debt. And it's about time we had a square deal.

True, the dedicated pipemen are in the minority. But it is a sizable minority. There are 1,750,000 of us who are loyal to the pipe alone.

The happy breed of pipemen, however, are social outcasts. Cigarette smokers are welcomed at restaurants and tightly packed parties. Pipe smokers most certainly are not. We trot along with our Billiard Chubby briars, our Bent Bulldogs, our Zulus, or our Squat Cads. We fill them with Black Twist or Honeydew, Rough Cut or Navy Cut, Bogie or Shag. We light up—and then wait for the hoary jeer.

'What are you burning in there—old socks?'

Once it might have been mildly amusing, I suppose. But this old hat (or, rather, old sock) crack begins to pall after you've heard it for the 17,000th time, I can tell you. The fact that the

49

pipeman can find cigarette fumes just as disagreeable is completely ignored.

Yet everything is laid on for the cigarette smokers. If they come to the end of a packet during the evening they can replenish stocks at any pub, club or restaurant. There are even bally machines hanging about the streets ready to serve them round the clock. No such luck for the pipeman. If he exhausts baccy supplies during the evening, he's done for.

Miserable ingratitude.

I say the traveller

By land, sea or air, travel broadens the mind—and the humour.
But I have been careful to avoid any imported Corn in this selection. It is all home-grown produce.

Captain boasting to woman passenger he has invited on to the
bridge of his ship:
'Yes, I know every sandbank and rock along this coast.'
Suddenly—a terrific crash. 'There you are, lady,' says the
captain. 'There's a big one for you.'
—Oi!

Woman driver speeding north on the motorway—and knitting.
A police patrolman catches her up and calls:
'Pull over!'
'No,' she says sweetly. 'Socks.'

'I say, conductor, do you stop at the Ritz?'
'What—on my wages?'

Elderly lady on her first flight peers out of the aircraft window
and says excitedly to the hostess:
'My—it's true! Those people down there do look just like
ants.'
'They *are* ants, madam. We haven't taken off yet.'

Country yokel tenders a £5 note at the station booking hall for
his big trip to the capital.
'Does the next train go to London?'
'That's right sir. Change at Reading.'
'I ain't waiting till I get to Reading, you give it to me now.'

Chap stumbles as he gets on the coach, and the driver inquires:

 'Did you bang your head?'
'No. I didn't know we had to.'

AA patrolman to woman driver parked in a lay-by:
 'Your trouble, madam, is the battery. It's flat.'
'Oh dear. What shape should it be then?'

Steward to cruise passenger:

 'Excuse me, sir. The captain invites you to sit at his table.'
'Not ruddy likely. You tell the captain that I didn't come on this cruise to sit with the crew.'

 'Pass farther down the train please.'
'That isn't father. It's my grandpa.'

Chap on a caravan touring holiday pulls up as he reaches the top of a steep hill, and seeks advice from an old lady standing at her garden gate.

 'Could you help me, please? Is this hill dangerous?'
'No, dear. Not here it isn't. It's down at the bottom they all crashes.'

Woman boards a country bus with ten nippers hanging round her skirt.
 'Are all these children yours, madam?' asks the driver. 'Or is it a picnic?'
'They're all mine, lad. And believe me, it's no picnic.'

 'I say, I felt awfully queasy on that train, sitting with my back to the engine.'
'Why didn't you ask the person opposite to change places?'
'I couldn't—there was no one there.'

 'Ladies and gentlemen, this is a recorded announcement. We welcome you aboard this flight and have pleasure in inform-

ing you that your trip will be entirely in the hands of the Automatic Pilot system. To ensure that you have a safe and smooth journey, the instruments will automatically adjust themselves to take care of any eventuality. We hope you enjoy your trip . . . your trip . . . your trip . . . your . . .'

Police motorcyclist overtakes a motorist and flags him down on a remote country road.

'Excuse me, sir. A lady who claims to be your wife fell out of your car about two miles back.'

'Thank goodness, officer! I thought I'd gone deaf.'

Lady on a voyage to the Middle East:

'Steward, can you tell me where the toilet is?'

'Yes, madam. Port side.'

'Good gracious. I don't think I can possibly wait till we get there.'

'I say, porter! How long will the next train be?'

'About six carriages, sir.'

'Smart, aren't you!'

'No, sir—I'm Jenkins. Smart's on strike.'

—Oi!

THE MAN YOU CAN'T TRUST

No doubt about it. This business of buying and selling cars is the supreme sourer of human relationships. Sadly, we live in an age when cynicism is the vogue. But we still try to give the benefit of the doubt to new acquaintances, don't we? Working on the same principle as Grand Old British Justice we assume that folk, by and large, are Good Eggs until they are proved Bad Eggs.

It is called our Faith in Human Nature.

There is one occasion, however, on which this commendable faith in H.N. is entirely absent. When we come face-to-face with a fellow human being about whom we know nothing, yet automatically believe him to be a wrong 'un.

When he is trying to sell us his motor car.

I have been embroiled in both buying and selling. And I am the lesser man for it.

It was, I felt, time for a change. So I polished my car to a finish it had never enjoyed since leaving the factory, and then pondered how much I should ask for it. This is a problem to which there is no ideal solution. Pitch the price too high and nobody will bother to look at your car. Pitch it too low and everybody will suspect grave hidden defects and will not touch it with a barge pole.

Why not settle for the happy medium? The answer to this is that it is impossible to decide what this 'happy medium' should be. And even if you do, by some lucky chance, hit it, you probably won't get it. Because of that wretched tradition of bargaining. Every customer assumes that you have inflated the asking price to allow for the certainty of its being knocked down.

So you're back to Square One again—pitching the price too high. And if you pitch the price too high nobody will bother to look at your car. . . .

After I had thought myself round to this point for the second time, I plumped for what I hoped might be a reasonably happy m.—and resolved to stand firm when the inevitable bargaining began. An ad was inserted in the local evening paper, and I waited for the calls to come pouring in. I got one. And that very evening, a stunningly attractive young lady arrived at the flat to inspect the vehicle.

Normally, one revels in making the acquaintance of stunningly attractive young ladies. And (with luck) they reciprocate. Not this time, though. She looked me straight in the eye and launched into the sort of intensive interrogation one would expect from the N.K.V.D. I avoided the stare, which was obviously meant to intimidate, and answered as best I could.

But it was no go. The stunner didn't trust me. I was a shark. She telephoned for the boy friend to come round and size up the situation. Soon he was nosing about the car, shaking his head and punctuating his inspection with irritating staccato sucks of breath through pursed lips.

56

Then the blighter started chipping away at the bottom of the car doors with a ball pen—and gave violent kicks to each of the tyres. This struck me as little short of vandalism. After all, it was still *my* car.

Inwardly I fumed. But what can you do? Just grin and bear it. Then the crunch. 'Not worth anywhere near what you're asking, of course, old boy.'

Absolute cheek. But again, what can you do? Two against one. Unmercifully they beat me down. I protested mildly, but had no stomach for the fight. The deal was clinched.

All right then. Now we know the form, on to Act II. In which Our Hero, armed with technique, should triumph.

I had already spotted, in the same newspaper that carried my ad, a motor I very much fancied. It had 'low mlge' and 'every extra'. It was a 'director's car' and in 'immac. cond.'

Director's car, eh? Just my style.

But after thinking it over, I wasn't so sure. You read about some very dodgy types who are company directors, don't you? I don't claim that our gaols are absolutely bursting with them, but you do hear from time to time that one has been sent down for fraud. Mmmmm . . . you can't be too careful, even with company directors.

Still, I pushed off to view the car and its owner.

The Director greeted me warmly with a palsy-walsy handshake. A mite too warm, I thought. And long sideburns. (If he's grown them since early 1969, fair enough. But if he's had them longer than that it quite definitely indicates shark qualities.)

He smiled a little too broadly as he reeled off the car's fine points. I tried the straight-in-the-eye ploy. No good. He stared me out. (Quite clearly a shark of the first water. He probably spends most of his waking hours conning innocents like me.)

The car, though, looked a beaut. It didn't have *every* extra, as advertised (no 007-type ejector seat, machine-guns or smoke-screen spewer) but it did have a radio. And the cond. certainly appeared to be immac.

Remembering my earlier lessons, I tried some desultory door-bottom chipping, although I couldn't bring myself to start aiming kicks at the tyres. But the Director was unimpressed.

We went for a trial spin. He pressed a switch. 'Radio—perfect, you see.' (A cunning move, that. Drowning tell-tale engine rumble, I'll be bound.)

Suddenly: 'Well, what do you think?'

I ought to get an expert to give the car the once-over. That's what I thought. But what I heard myself saying was 'I'll take it'. And I didn't even have a stab at knocking down the price.

Since then, I've lived on my nerve ends. Each time the ear picks up the slightest rumble or squeak the heart stops. Is this *it*? Everything *may* be fine. And my Director *may* be one of the most honest fellows with whom you could hope to do business.

But he has sold me a second-hand car.

And though, deep down, we may know we are being unfair, we just don't trust people who sell us second-hand cars.

I say ❦ at the quack's

Doctors, dentists and opticians have always been a rewarding source of Corn—with the family G.P. the clear favourite. But it is mostly the patient, rather than the doctor, who is the butt of the jokes. Or if the doc is the butt, he is usually let down pretty lightly. Which may be an indication of the high esteem in which he is held by the community. That, at any rate, will be an assumption with which your local G.P. will not quarrel.

To redress this unequal balance, let us commence with a couple of grand exceptions. . . .

❦ Doctor: *'I'm afraid I can't diagnose your complaint. It must be the drink.'*
'O.K., doc—I'll come back when you're sober.'
—Oi!

❦ 'Did that medicine I gave your uncle straighten him out?'
'Yes, doctor, they buried him yesterday.'

Patient with two broken ribs:
❦ *'Doctor, I keep getting this stitch in my side.'*
'Fine—that shows the bones are knitting.'

❦ 'I say, doctor—my hair keeps falling out. Can you recommend anything to keep it in?'
'Certainly. Perhaps this empty cigar box may be of use.'

❦ *'Doctor, I get this terrible pain in my back every time I bend.'*
'Then don't bend. Next patient.'

59

Chinese chap with toothache telephones for a dental appointment, asking:

 'What time you fix?'

'2.30 all right?' inquires the dentist.

'Tooth-hurty all right, but what time you fix?'

An optician is examining a glam. blonde.

 'Have your eyes been checked before?'

'No, darling—they've always been blue.'

Same glam. blonde, this time having her tummy examined by the doctor, who tells her:

 'You'll have to diet.'

'What colour, doctor?'

 'I say, I say! I'm off to the doctor. Feel a bit giddy.'

'Vertigo?'

'No—just round the corner.'

Chap with an inferiority complex pours his heart out.

 'Doctor, doctor—nobody notices me.'

'Next patient, please.'

 'Doctor, I get this stabbing pain in my eye every time I have a cup of tea.'

'Try taking the spoon out.'

 'I say, I say! The doc said I could get rid of my cold by drinking freezing orange juice after a hot bath.'

'Really? Got rid of it yet?'

'No—I haven't finished drinking the hot bath.'

 'Doctor, I talk in my sleep.'

'Well, that's not so terrible.'

'I know. But I'm such a bore.'

🎵 'I say, reckon old Bill will be in hospital for some time yet.'
'Why, seen his doctor?'
'No, seen his nurse.'

🎵 *'I used to be so conceited that I had to see a psychiatrist. Now after only three months' treatment I'm one of the nicest fellows you could wish to meet.'*

🎵 'How do you like the new doctor, Mavis?'
'Oh, he's ever so sympathetic. He makes you feel really ill.'

Worried chap nursing broken finger:
🎵 *'When it heals, doctor, will I be able to play the piano?'*
'Of course you will.'
'That's marvellous—I never could before.'
—Oi!

EES MEAT

Eating out these days presents a growing challenge: how to get your message across. For I'm sure you will agree that it is becoming increasingly difficult to find waiters with a working knowledge of our lingo.

No problem with home-grown waiters, of course. And no problem with foreign waiters either—if the menu is in the Mother Tongue. You simply point to what you want and the waiter buzzes off to get it. What he orders from the chef may not sound like what you ordered, but there is a fair chance that it will turn out to be one and the same.

It is in continental restaurants—and by this I do not necessarily mean 'The Continent', but any continent—that problems can arise. There can be a complete breakdown in communication. For they delight in foxing you with fancy names. You don't understand the menu. And the waiter doesn't understand you.

The Chinese restaurant more or less solves the problem by numbering every dish (damned clever, these fiendish Chinese) and thus leaving little to chance. Some Indians do this too—and in any case they have the edge, because in the old Empire days we conned them into learning our language, rather than taking the trouble to learn theirs. The real trouble comes when you decide to dine at one of those French bistros or Italian trattorias. Particularly the trats.

Poring over a trat menu the other night I spotted *Scallopine antica Roma con ciliege*. Quite a mouthful, you'll agree. But a mouthful of what? Clearly the dish had originated in ancient Rome, but more than that I could not divine. So I consulted the waiter.

Now, long ago, Italian waiters earned a very special reputation with their undoubted ability to Make You Feel At Home. And though the wing collars and tails have been replaced by neckerchieves and striped sweaters, the welcome is just as warm. If not warmer. Today's lot tend to overdo things by piling 'Bella-bellas' on to the bird one has in tow. (A bit irritating that can be, but I suppose one must allow these Latins a little licence. After all, as I mutter to the Bird in Tow, it's a load of old flannel—and, anyway, who's paying the bill?)

But although modern Italian waiters may be strong on the Big Hello, they are not, in the main, strong on language. I assume they speak Italian excellently—were I in a position to confirm this I would not have stumbled over *Scallopine antica Roma con ciliege*, of course—but they really ought to ease up on the 'Bella-bellas' and concentrate on boning up their English.

This brings us back to that night at the trat. For when I pointed to *Scallopine antica Roma con ciliege* and posed the question 'What is this?', our waiter clearly failed.

'Ees very good, sir,' he said.

'I'm sure it's very good' (not that waiters—Italian or otherwise—ever tell you anything is lousy) 'but what is it?'

The waiter's brow creased. The poor fellow cocked his head and stared intently at us, searching for clues. You know the expression—most dogs adopt it when you're giving them a gentle lecture and they can't quite get the drift of what you're saying.

Then he brightened, and beamed with relief. He'd got it. By George, he'd got it!

'Ees meat, sir.'

What a shame. He hadn't got it after all. I tried again.

'Yes, I know ees—er, it's—meat, but have you any other details?'

'That's right, sir. *Scallopine antica Roma con ciliege.*'

And he scampered off to the kitchen to get the chef weaving. No chance to call him back. And no point, either, I suppose. Just have to take pot luck.

When it arrived, *Scallopine antica Roma con ciliege* turned out to be slices of veal cooked in butter with cherries and madeira sauce. And jolly tasty it was too. Make a note of it. But one man's meat, etc. . . . I could have been landed with some foul dish I didn't fancy at all.

So I applaud a scheme operated by Britain's biggest hotel group, Trust House Forte, for waiters in their London establishments, which comprise smooth joints like Grosvenor House and Quaglino's. They have put their foreign staff through a rudimentary linguistic test. Those who fail have been sent on a course of language lessons.

It is a step in the right direction. Meanwhile for your delight, I pass on an example of what they are up against—even at first-class hotels.

The group's training officer told me that one evening a waiter was wandering about with a plate bearing two fried eggs and a kipper.

'An odd combination, even for breakfast,' mused the head waiter, who had observed him. 'But who on earth has been ordering two eggs and a kipper at this time of night?'

The head waiter made some enquiries and tracked down the

customer concerned, sitting with two companions. It turned out that they had actually asked for two whiskies and a cherry brandy.

How come then, that they were being served with two eggs and a kipper?

The customer repeated his order: 'Two Haigs and De Kuyper.'

I say 🥕 eating out

Part I

We are in debt to the humble waiter. He provides the raw material for more corny jokes than dogs, policemen, doctors, golfers, women drivers, topers—even mothers-in-law. I am not able to explain why he should be so pre-eminent in the field of Corn. But pre-eminent he certainly is.

Now, you may conclude from Part I of the selection below that, apart from the odd exception, waiters are portrayed as a lily-livered lot. It may appear that they are a pathetic, downtrodden crew who serve merely as sounding boards for the puny witticisms of arrogant diners. Not a bit of it.

Part II will present 'The Grand Waiter-Fly-And-Soup Marathon', starring the waiter in a far from humble role—demonstrating that, in a corny world, a waiter can give as good as he gets. And then some.

So don't waste your sympathy on those 'who only stand and wait'.

🥕 *'I say, waiter—there's a worm on my dinner.'*
'Sir! That is fat.'
'I should think so. It's eaten all the meat.'
—Oi!

🥕 'How did you find the steak, sir?'
'Oh, I just moved a potato and there it was.'

🥕 *'Hey, waiter! Call the manager. I can't eat this terrible food.'*
'What's the use, sir? He wouldn't eat it either.'

Chap goes into a milk bar and asks the husky-voiced girl assistant for a sample of their ices.

 'Certainly, sir,' whispers the girl. 'Which sort?'
'I say, have you laryngitis?'
'No, sir, only strawberry and vanilla.'

 'Waiter—my boiled egg is bad.'
'I'm sorry, sir—I only laid the table.'

 'I say, waiter—do you serve crabs in this restaurant?'
'We serve anyone, sir. Sit down.'

 'I asked for a nice lobster, waiter. How come you brought me one with only one claw?'
'So maybe it was in a fight, sir.'
'So maybe you bring me the winner?'

Diner leans over to the chap at the next table:
 'Do they serve snails here?'
'No, they disguise them as waiters.'

 'I say, waiter, I don't like this cheese.'
'But it's Gruyère, sir.'
'Well, bring me some that grew somewhere else.'

An old boy tucking into the turkey during the firm's Christmas party held at a local hotel suddenly plunges both hands into the stuffing and rubs it vigorously into his hair. Puzzled chap opposite remarks:

 'That was quite extraordinary. Why did you rub that sage-and-onion stuffing into your hair?'
'Sage-and-onion stuffing?' the old boy exclaims. 'Good Heavens! I thought it was sausage meat.'

 'I say, waiter—have you any wild duck?'
'No, sir. But we have a tame one we could aggravate for you.'

68

'Waiter—I'd like a nice juicy steak.'
'Yes, sir. A 50p one or a 75p one?'
'What's the difference?'
'Well, no difference. But for 75p you get a sharper knife.'

'Hey, waiter! Have you any stewed prunes?'
'Yes, sir.'
'Well, give 'em some black coffee to sober 'em up.'

'I say, waiter—do you have frogs' legs?'
'Certainly, sir.'
'Good—hop over the counter and get me a cheese sandwich.'
—Oi!

I say 🐝 eating out

Part 2: The Grand Waiter-Fly-And-Soup Marathon

Yes folks! At last it's the 'Grand Waiter-Fly-And-Soup Marathon'. Presented for the first time in the public prints (could just possibly be a false boast, but that's showman's licence). HEAR the diners roar as they discover the fly! DELIGHT in the nimble ripostes of the waiters! DRINK the soup! EAT (if you choose) the insect!

The diner who bawls 'Waiter, there's a fly in my soup!' is meat and drink to the Corny Jokester. He is the gagman's copy-book feed. 'Waiter, there's a fly in my soup!' surpasses, in my opinion, 'Why did the chicken cross the road?', 'Who was that lady I saw you with last night?' and all the rest, as the most prolific straight line in the history of Corn.

Ladies and Gentlemen! Sit back in your seats for safety and comfort. Extinguish your cigarettes. Fasten your safety belts. (On second thoughts, unfasten your safety belts.) And stand by for . . . ACTION!

🐝 'Waiter, there's a fly in my soup.'
'Yes, sir—better sip it with care.'

🐝 *'Waiter, there's a fly in my soup.'*
'Just a moment, sir—I'll fetch a spider.'

🐝 'Waiter, there's a fly in my soup.'
'Keep your voice down, sir—they'll all want one.'

🐝 *'Waiter, there's a fly in my soup.'*
'That will be another 3p, sir.'

'Waiter, what's this fly doing in my soup?'
'Dunno, sir—looks like the breast stroke.'

'Waiter, there's a fly in my soup.'
'Nonsense, sir—we don't serve meat on Fridays.'

'Waiter—there's a fly in my soup.'
'Don't worry, sir—he's only showing off.'

'Waiter, there's a fly in my soup.'
'Funny—it's supposed to be mock-turtle.'

'Waiter, there's a fly in my soup.'
'Yes, sir—the chef used to be a tailor.'

'Waiter, there's a fly in my soup.'
'Not to worry, sir—he's a good swimmer.'

'Waiter, there's a fly in my soup.'
'Hang on—I'll call the R.S.P.C.A.'

'Waiter, there's a fly in my soup.'
'Sorry—it should be in the Cornish pasty.'

'Waiter, there's a fly swimming in my soup.'
'You're lucky, sir—there's usually only enough for them to paddle.'

'Waiter, there's a dead fly swimming in my soup.'
'Nonsense, sir—dead flies can't swim.'

'Waiter, there's a fly in my soup.'
'That's all right, sir—no extra charge.'

'Waiter, there's a dead fly floating in my soup.'
'Yes, sir—it's the hot water that kills them.'

'Waiter, there's a fly in my soup.'
'Don't worry, sir—it won't drink much.'

And finally:

 'Waiter, I don't like all these flies floating in my soup.'
*'Well, tell me which ones you do like, sir, and I'll fish the
others out.'*
—Oi!

YOUR FATE IN THE STARS?

Tosh is the word for astrology. Quite riveting, but absolute tosh. Most people—me included—cannot resist scanning their horoscopes in newspapers and magazines. And a fair-sized proportion believes that there could, at least, be something to them.

Not I. My mind is ever open, but in the absence of conclusive evidence to the contrary I declare: Astrology is Bunk.

Look at those character analyses. They are read eagerly by

millions, for we all find ourselves fascinating, don't we? You love reading about you. And I love reading about me.

At the newsagent's, my eyes lit upon a horoscope booklet written by one of Britain's best-known astrologers. I couldn't resist buying it, and I must admit that I frequently muttered 'Hear! Hear!' as I read what he had to say about folk born under my sign.

According to this astrologer, I am *a natural humanitarian, industrious, a peacemaker, generous, sympathetic, popular, very courteous, extremely intuitive, highly sensitive, generally artistic and harmonious, usually gifted with good looks, and very sociable.*

My mind is *flexible and creative* and my faculties as a theatre critic are *high*. I also have *a natural rhythm*, which makes me *a graceful dancer*.

Mister Perfect? Well, not quite. There are minor qualifications —like 'Perhaps at times you need a little more sense of humour' (most folk would say I've got a damn sight too much)—but it is a glowing portrait. I like it. I like it. Absolutely spot-on as far as I am concerned. Although I can hardly believe it applies to *all* my fellows born under this sign.

But I am a suspicious cove. I bought eleven more horoscope books dealing with the other Signs of the Zodiac. (People don't usually do this. They read their own and ignore the others.) And when I started reading what the astrologer had to say about the remaining eleven-twelfths of the population, I found more glowing portraits.

There were some differences and qualifications, but it was the similarities that were striking. Here, for instance, is what the astrologer says about physical appearances:

CAPRICORN (December 22–January 20): Attractive. (Women 'often beautiful' and men 'often gifted with the looks of an Adonis'.)
PISCES (February 20–March 20): Large expressive eyes—a gift conferred by your planet Neptune.
TAURUS (April 21–May 21): Probably gifted with good looks.

74

GEMINI (May 22–June 21): Gifted with almost eternal youth.
CANCER (June 22–July 23): Usually gifted with good looks.
VIRGO (August 24–September 23): Often endowed with looks much younger than their age.
LIBRA (September 24–October 23): Usually gifted with good looks.
SCORPIO (October 24–November 22): Invariably good looks.
SAGITTARIUS (November 23–December 21): Classic—almost godlike—good looks.

Wow! That deals with three-quarters of the population. They should be well satisfied, to say the least.

The books do not appear to mention the looks of those born under AQUARIUS (January 21–February 19), ARIES (March 21–April 20), or LEO (July 24–August 23). Perhaps they were sold short when good looks were being dished out!

Another curious thing is that, according to the stars, nearly everybody turns out to love the theatre or the cinema—news which may puzzle managers who have been complaining for years about audiences lost to the telly.

Everybody is, almost invariably, 'courteous'. And nearly everybody is popular. (The astrologer says Virgoans may be at a 'slight disadvantage' because it is 'possible' they may scare some people away with their rather cold façades. But they do have 'natural magnetic charm'. Which should make up for that 'slight disadvantage'.)

What really makes me chortle is the description of our homes. In the Capricorn house you can expect to find 'elegance and taste', and an Aquarian's is 'usually extremely tastefully decorated'. A Piscean's taste is 'usually impeccable', and the home of an Arian, whose taste is 'usually rather extravagant', looks 'clean and extremely smart'. The Taurian house is 'kept spotlessly clean', the Gemini house is 'invariably spotlessly clean', and so is that of the Cancerian, who has 'extremely good taste' and is 'always a stickler for cleanliness'. In the Leo home, where 'all has to be light and airy', there is 'well-designed furniture'. And the Virgo home

—'clean and tidy in every detail'—has 'impeccable furniture' too. Librans have 'extremely good taste' in their homes, which are kept 'spotlessly clean'. Scorpio houses are 'full of good quality furniture' and will 'always be clean'. And what will the Sagittarian's home be like? Full marks—it will 'always be clean'.

If cleanliness is next to godliness, we must all be doing pretty well. Particularly those Sagittarians who have 'almost godlike good looks' to boot!

I suppose the stars do influence us to a mild extent. 'Good day for meeting old friends' you read. So you make it come true by enjoying the day looking up old friends. But then it's always pleasant to meet old friends. Or 'Take care over money' (sound advice at any time). Or 'Keep your eyes open this afternoon' (presumably to avoid bumping into people).

Good tips. But quite hopeless as a guide to what may actually happen. I mean, you never read anything really useful like 'Look in the gutter at the corner of High Street and Market Road this evening, and you'll find a fiver.' That *would* be something!

If you do want to get an inkling of what the future has in store, I recommend you to stop monkeying around with astrological charts and invite you, instead, to employ my method of prediction —'What The Parsnips Foretell' (Patents Pending).

Obtain, and scrape, two large parsnips. Around one, place slips of paper bearing predictions for the year ahead. You should combine intelligent anticipation, and generalized forecasts that are almost bound to come up, with the odd long shot. (You'll get the idea from a quick look at astrologers' predictions for previous years.) Around the other parsnip, place more slips—some giving the months, and some saying 'Yes' or 'No'.

All you do is spin the parsnips and record the results.

What The Parsnips Foretell may not always prove to be *absolutely* accurate. But I have found them to be more accurate than the Stars.

So do give the parsnips a whirl.

I say 🐝 and the law

All characters in these legal jokes are fictitious. Any resemblance between them and policemen, customs officers, lawyers, magistrates or judges—living or dead—is entirely coincidental. (No point in asking for trouble, is there?)

Magistrate to prisoner in the dock:
🐝 '*Is this the first time you've been up before me?*'
'*I don't know, Your Worship. What time do you normally get up?*'
—Oi!

🐝 'If you are a police officer, why are you wearing that black and white patterned suit?'
'Oh, it's just a routine check, sir.'

🐝 *Judge: 'So you and your wife have been fighting again? Liquor, I suppose?*'
'*No, sir. She licked me this time.*'

A solicitor reassures his farmer client.
🐝 'Don't worry, I'll get you off all right.'
'Would it help if I sent the judge a couple of ducks?'
'Good heavens, no! It would go against you.'
After the case has been heard, the solicitor shakes the farmer's hand: 'There you are. Said you'd get off.'
'I know. I sent the ducks in the other chap's name.'

Chap goes into a police station and tells the duty sergeant:
☙ *'I should like to report that my mother-in-law is missing.'*
'So should I, sir. So should I.'

☙ WITNESS : 'He was as drunk as a judge.'
JUDGE : 'You mean drunk as a lord.'
WITNESS : 'Yes, my Lord.'

Policeman taking statement from woman driver after crash:
☙ *'Whose fault was it, madam?'*
'I don't really know, officer. I wasn't looking.'

Judge to truculent barrister :
☙ 'Are you trying to show contempt for this court?'
'No, m'Lord. I am doing my best to conceal it.'

An old boy is asked by the Customs if he has anything to declare.
☙ *'No—nothing at all.'*
'What's in this bottle, sir?'
'Only holy water from Lourdes.'
The Customs officer pulls the cork, takes a sniff, and pronounces: 'This is whisky.'
'Glory be to God. A miracle.'

Policeman to lady after crash:
☙ 'May I see your driving licence, madam?'
'Don't be silly, constable. Who would give *me* one?'

Judge to burglar up in court for the third time:
☙ *'Why is it that every time you've been caught you've been robbing a third-floor flat?'*
'Well, your Honour, that's my storey and I'm sticking to it'.

Policeman accosts a fellow weaving unsteadily along the street at
2 a.m.

'Now then, sir. Where are you going?'
'To a lecture, offisher. To a lecture.'
'And who,' inquires the Law, 'is giving a lecture at this time of night?'
'My wife, offisher. My wife.'
—*Oi!*

TONGUE TWISTER

Mrs Timmans put out her tongue, upside down. I had known her
for just seven minutes. Yet here was this attractive young wife
and mother sticking her tongue out at me.

It happened when I popped into 'The Plough' for a few evening
jars with friends. We were chatting at the bar when in walked the

remarkable Mrs T. with her husband. I'd never been privileged to meet her before, but she knew my companions, and they effected an introduction.

Precisely how we arrived at the Tongue Incident, I don't quite know. It had something to do with our discussion about hereditary influences. We were recalling a survey which indicated that sixty-four per cent of the population can roll their tongues into a U-shape, while the rest cannot.

Anyway, Mrs Timmans stopped us in our tracks with this proud question: 'But can you do *this*?'

That was when she stuck her tongue out upside down.

It looks easy enough. But it is not. I will pause while *you* have a go. . . .

See? I expect you couldn't get anywhere near it. Neither could we. Mrs T. had us all at it, beaming triumphantly as we tried, tried and tried again. But always our tongues came out the right way up. I even attempted to cheat by grasping the tip of my tongue with thumb and forefinger—quite a feat in itself—and twisting it round. Without success.

An interesting and frustrating experiment. And at the time I thought that the remarkable Mrs T. stood alone. But during the next few days I discovered that there were others who could manage the Timmans Tongue Twister. (It would appear that it is primarily a female accomplishment. Few men can work the trick. How does one account for this peculiar example of Woman's Superiority? Could it be that she gives her tongue a little more exercise than we do?)

This sort of thing takes you back to early school-days when status was measured entirely by achievements such as these. 'Can you crack your fingers? Can you waggle your ears? Can you whistle through your teeth? Can you raise one eyebrow? Well, I can—so there!'

My own particular forte was a klaxon horn effect, which could scare the living daylights (whatever they are) out of anyone within a 25-yard radius—*and still can.*

Now we are adult. We don't go in for this sort of thing as a rule. We reserve our boasting for more solid achievements. After all, what advantages does it bring you—or anyone else—to be able to stick out your tongue upside down? None, you say. And you may be quite right.

But I fancy I see one possible beneficiary. Although Master Timmans is only two years old at present, it should not be long before he is the envy of his pals. For few boys could better the boast: '*My* mother can put her tongue out upside down!'

I say ⚇ for sporting types

In my experience, the best source of sporting Corn is golf. Though why this should be so I cannot hazard. It is just possible that it could have something to do with the popularity of the convivial 'Nineteenth Hole'. Victims of club-house bores may have devised the jokes to relieve the tedium—as sparkling chasers to pep up a long, and exceedingly flat, drink. Possible. But I doubt it. For every sport has its share of bores. And, by and large, golfers don't invent the golfing jokes—any more than mothers-in-law invent mother-in-law jokes.

Let us begin, though, with a *non*-golfing ear of Corn which is particularly versatile.

A chap is dancing with a somewhat snooty partner—and making rather a hash of things.

⚇ 'I say, you must forgive me. I'm afraid I'm a little stiff from rugby.'

'I don't care where you come from—you won't dance with me again.'

(Particularly versatile, as I say, because it can be adapted to suit a variety of sports. He need not necessarily be a little stiff from Rugby. He can be a little stiff from Badminton. Or from Bowling, near Glasgow. Or even, at a pinch, from Saling, near Braintree, Essex.)

⚇ '*I say, I say! Why does Tony Jacklin wear two pairs of trousers?*'

'*In case he gets a hole in one.*'

—Oi!

84

Two cats chatting as they watch progress on the Centre Court at Wimbledon.

🎗 'I say—I didn't realize you were so interested in tennis.'
'I'm not. It's just that my old man's in the racket.'

Chap all togged up in riding gear, accosts a stable hand:
🎗 *'I say—can I hire this horse?'*
'Certainly, sir. You'll find there's a little screw under the saddle.'

Exchange in a football crowd:
🎗 'Hey—who do you think you're shoving?'
'Dunno mate—what's your name?'

🎗 *'Why don't you play golf with Colonel Gadsby any more?'*
'Well, would you play golf with a man who cheats, falsifies his score, and moves the ball out of the rough when your back is turned?'
'Of course not.'
'Neither will Colonel Gadsby.'

Chap is leaning on a gate at Newmarket, when a horse trots up and whispers:
'I won the Derby last year.' Disconcerted, the fellow moves on to another gate. But the horse follows him and repeats his whispered boast. So feeling in need of a restoring brandy, the chap finds a pub and tells one of the locals about the talking horse.
🎗 'Oh yes. Did he tell you he won the Derby last year?'
'That's right.'
'Well, he's a ruddy liar. He only came in second.'

Gamekeeper spots an angler reeling them in from the syndicate's stretch of the river.
🎗 *'Can't you read? That notice says "PRIVATE—No Fishing".'*
'Oh, but I wouldn't be so rude as to read a private notice.'

Little girl watches a golfer trying to get out of a bunker.

☙ 'Well, Daddy, he's stopped beating it now. I think it must be dead.'

☙ *'The wife's coming with me to the match on Saturday.'*
'Soccer?'
'No need, she wants to.'

A horsebox arrives at the racecourse. But when the stable lads open the doors they call to the driver:

☙ 'Hoy! This box is empty!'
'I know that. But *somebody* has to bring the non-runners.'

A tramp dozing in a bunker on the golf course is discovered by the club secretary, who boots him none too gently and tells him to clear off.

☙ *'And who,'* demands the tramp, *'are you?'*
'I am the secretary of this club.'
'Well,' snorts the tramp, *'that's no way to get new members.'*
—Oi!

MOTORING—WAR OR PEACE?

When a motorist does wrong, don't try to 'teach him a lesson'. This is the advice of the government manual on driving, which warns us never to motor in the spirit of retaliation. It is sound. I Know It Makes Sense. But it is jolly difficult advice to follow.

If some wretched driver is behaving like a maniac, it requires a will of iron to resist retaliation. I've always felt that retaliation is, in some cases, almost a public duty. Not just a question of getting one's own back.

The other night I was driving along the outside lane towards

Marble Arch. I observed through my mirror that a car was fast catching up on me—going like the clappers. Already I was slightly above the speed limit, but the car behind closed the gap between us and began flashing its lights furiously.

Behaving like a maniac, in fact.

Well, the road was busy and I couldn't easily pull over. And anyway, I felt the maniac would likely cause a nasty accident if he was allowed to go on at that rate. So began a lengthy and hair-raising dice, with the flashing maniac clinging to my tail, and me trying to fulfil my public duty and 'teach him a lesson' by dabbing my brake pedal.

Finally, he swung out and began to overtake *in the oncoming lane*. Good grief—a *real* maniac!

But it wasn't. It was the police.

That (I thought as I was waved to the side of the road) has torn it. But while the two constables were striding grimly towards me, I decided they deserved a bit of stick. I launched into a tirade and accused them of being a menace on the roads. And of driving like maniacs. Adding, for good measure, that they ought to be ashamed of themselves.

Just where my confidence came from, I don't know. But it quite took the wind out of the constabulary sails. I was let off with a caution that it was *their* job to police the roads, not mine. I agreed —and promised not to do it again.

But in apportioning the blame for retaliatory and aggressive motoring, the car manufacturers themselves must not be allowed to escape. The labels they give to some of their creations are hardly pacific: Avenger, Jaguar, Rapier, Interceptor, Stiletto, Scimitar, etc. Mount one of those and you are riding a war-horse.

Shortly after my hair-raising dice on the Road to Marble Arch, however, it struck me that car labels can also be a power for peace and goodwill.

Now and again, I find myself driving with exquisite courtesy, giving way, with a cheery wink and a wave, to motorists and pedestrians alike. The explanation can be found on a thin label stuck across my car windscreen.

Now, normally I abhor windscreen stickers. They can be dangerous because they obscure your view of what is going on outside your little tin box. But my sticker is quite definitely a Spur to Good Driving. It is a call for everyone to support the party which gets my vote at each election. (No need to say which party this is. When I tell you it is the party for which any really intelligent and well-informed citizen would vote, you will recognize it instantly.)

In my constituency—yours too, probably—the party needs all the votes it can get. Unfortunately I can supply it with one only. So I naturally want to persuade as many waverers as possible to rally to the cause. Hence the sticker.

And hence the Exquisite Courtesy. For I reckon that those floating voters who benefit from my Exquisite C., and observe my cheery winking and waving, might possibly think: 'Any party that gets the vote of that fine fellow gets my vote too!'

The sniggety-snag, though, is that I also have to suffer vulgar abuse from the committed voters of the other parties, who wind down their windows to give me an earful as they flash by.

It is difficult to refrain from retaliating. Especially as, but for my sticker, I would be first in the Vulgar Abuse Stakes (*vide* 'Talking Politics' which follows). But refrain I do, giving the same cheery waves and winks in the hope that they may later regret their unseemly behaviour and, as a penance, plump for the party advertised in my car window.

This has brought home to me the enormous millstone that hangs round the neck of your average van-driver. When you think about it, he has a much more responsible job than, say, a firm's advertising man. For unless he is fortunate enough to drive a plain van, the '*Gadsby's Frozen Spare-Ribs are World-beaters*' sign makes him a roving ambassador for his employer.

If that van-driver tears around cutting up other motorists and aggrieved drivers follow through with a stiff letter to his boss, well—it could mean the chop from Gadsby's Frozen Spare-Ribs Ltd. And it may well hit the company's business.

Lest you think this is fanciful, I must tell you that nine years ago I had a narrow squeak as the result of appalling driving by a chap behind the wheel of a van loaded with—and clearly labelled as containing—my favourite brand of sausages.

I have refused, on principle, to buy those sausages ever since.

I say ❦ the mean Scots

Before we go any further, let me make it clear that I regard the title of this chapter as a bit of a cheat. It could certainly be held as a *prima facie* libel.

The jokes that follow have one thing in common—a mean streak. And I ask you—is it just to claim that the Scots are mean? I have no way of ascertaining what the majority verdict would be. But I guess most people would say that the Scottish reputation for stinginess is ill-founded.

The Scots, however, have only themselves to blame for their reputation. For the bulk of them go out of their way to foster it. Maybe they are making the best of a bad job by taking a perverse delight in emphasizing a dubious national characteristic. At all events, it doesn't seem to worry them overmuch.

My experience has been that they fail dismally to live down to their reputation. That is why I suggest this chapter is a cheat. Still, if you do think the Scots are mean, take these jokes at their face value.

Alternatively, you may transfer them to the Jews—who run neck-and-neck with the Scots in revelling in mean reputations (equally undeserved in my view)—or the Welsh or the Irish or the English. Or, indeed, any minority group that tickles your fancy.

To do this, unfortunately, would mean losing a lot in the translation. So I recommend you to enjoy them as they come.

The Scots do.

Fergus calls on his best friend Jock and is surprised to find him peeling off the wallpaper in the sitting-room.
❦ *'Och! I didna ken you were decorating, Jock.'*
   'Na, na, Fergie. I'm moving.'

'You didna tell me Angus lost his luggage.'
'Aye, he did.'
'How was that?'
'The cork came oot.'

Outside Aberdeen post office:
 'Aye, Sandy. Ye've been puttin' mair money in the savings bank, eh?'
'Na, Donal. Just been in fillin' ma fountain pen.'

The Baillie addresses the defendant in a matrimonial court.
 'I am going to allow your wife £5 a week.'
'Thank you very much, sir. I'll try to gi'e her a few bob mysel'.'

Fergus goes into a pub and orders a pint of 1929 ale. This flummoxes the barman who asks the landlord what he should do about this strange request.
 'Draw him one oot of the pumps,' hisses the landlord. 'He'll no' ken the difference.'
The barman complies and gives the customer his pint. Fergus fumbles in his pocket, hands the barman five old pennies, and says: 'Thanks verra much. I didna think you'd have any left.'

Donal bumps into Jock in London's Oxford Street.
 'Jock! What are you doing here?'
'I'm on my honeymoon.'
'Ah, aye. Where's your wife—shopping?'
'Na, na. She didna come. She was here on her holidays last year.'

 'Och, Jamie. Why are you wearing your troosers inside oot?'
'It's the only pair I have. And there's holes in the other side.'

Winnie puts the Big Question to Sandy after they've been courting for twenty years.

🌱 'Do you not think it's time we got married?'
'Aye, Winnie. But who would have us now?'

The Minister sees old Sandy walking along leaning heavily on a
very short stick.
🌱 'Hallo there, Sandy. *That rheumatism troubling you again?*'
'*No—I broke ma stick.*'

Two mourners are talking after the funeral.
🌱 'Ah weel, that's auld Sandy laid to rest. They say he left twa
thoosan.'
'Sandy never left it. He was ta'en awa' frae it.'

Sandy finally arrives at heaven. St Peter meets him at the gates
and asks his nationality.
🌱 '*I'm a Scot.*'
'*Then you can't come in. We cannot make porridge for one.*'

A solicitor tells his client:
🌱 'Weel, your Uncle Sandy did remember you in his will
after a'.'
'He did?'
'Aye. He didna leave you anything.'
—Och!

STATUS SYMBOL

The one-up luxury of colour television is mine (he crowed). For less than a pound a week I have rented a splendid little portable.

One aspect of the deal, though, puzzled me. When I came to sign the rental agreement, the chap asked a rather surprising—and seemingly irrelevant—question: 'Are you married?'

Well, no. Why? But he couldn't explain. 'It's just a question we have to ask,' he said.

As I relaxed in an armchair, soaking up the glorious colour, the question kept nagging me. What if I had been married? Would that have disqualified me? ('I'm sorry, sir—you mustn't be greedy. You have a wife. You can't expect to have colour television as well.')

Surely that couldn't be it. Yet what other explanation was there? To discover the answer I telephoned a representative of the rental company.

'It's a routine question to help establish your credit rating,' he explained. 'More than half Britain's television sets are rented—it's a very big business. And married people tend to be more stable.'

Did this mean that Harold Wilson, married for more than thirty years, would be regarded as a safer proposition than bachelor Edward Heath?

'Well, no. The question is primarily directed at the women.'

So single women are less reliable than married women?

'As credit risks in general—yes, I'm afraid so,' said the rep. 'When they are married it does mean there should be at least one substantial wage-earner in the household.'

Then a spinster would find it more difficult than a bachelor to hire colour TV?

'Not necessarily. But the company would probably have to pay rather more attention to her financial circumstances. After all, women do, in the main, earn less than men.'

Yes—it's certainly tough for the single girls. But never let it be said that I would ignore a worthy cause. Unselfishly, I hereby invite them round to my flat for an evening's colour television. One at a time, of course.

Given this extra bonus afforded by colour TV, my life should be complete bliss. But one million Britons are guilty of rubbing the gilt from my gingerbread. I refer to the licence dodgers.

A colour licence, quite reasonably, costs more than a black-and-white one. I do not grudge paying the extra charge (especially in view of that bonus for bachelors!) but it does make a tidy hole in the pocket. And if you are one of those who have 'forgotten' to shell out for a TV licence—be it for colour or black-and-white —I hope your ears are burning. Were it not for you, the hole in my pocket would be less 'tidy'.

The majority of us do the decent thing and, however grudgingly, pay up. Those who don't do the decent thing may be nabbed by the pale blue detector vans, bristling with intimidating electronic equipment, which comb the country winkling out the backsliders.

Although it is the B.B.C. which benefits from the licence fees, commercials have been screened on rival I.T.V. in an attempt to shame the licence dodgers. But if the lads at the Corporation had the wit to see it, they have the remedy in their own hands.

Secure in the knowledge that I have a licence for my set, I offer them this weapon with my compliments: A great new peak-time B.B.C.-T.V. series—*The Detectors*. Powerful stuff pointing the moral that to evade the licence fee is to board the express train to Hell. . . .

'*SOCIETY must be ever vigilant against its enemies! And when these enemies number one million, the man chosen to hit back must be resolute, ruthless. Such a man is Chief Detector Eliot Ness. His hand-picked team of dedicated operators, indomitable in their ceaseless search for licence dodgers everywhere, are the Knights of the Twentieth Century. They are known throughout the land as . . . THE DETECTORS.*'

A family sits fitfully watching television. Each member is in fear. For their set is unlicensed. They take it in turns to keep a vigil at the front window. But, for a moment, the look-out's eyes stray to the screen—leaving the street outside unobserved. A fatal slip. Brakes screech and The Detectors leap from their blue van and race up the garden path. One takes the front door, the other covers the back.

Exposure. Oh! the shame of it. And perhaps—for good measure —ruin for the family breadwinner who cannot pay the £50 fine.

Gripping entertainment for those of us who can enjoy it with clear consciences. And a sure-fire method of winkling out the evaders and sending them racing to the nearest post office.

I say ❦ man's best friends

The dog, more than any other pet, is the Corny Jokester's best friend. The remaining domestic pets hardly rate at all.

Budgies and parrots win a place—largely, I suppose, because of their mastery of the language. (On this basis, I dare say that if golden hamsters could talk they could squeeze in too. But they can't, so they can't.)

In view of the dog's popularity as a subject for corny jokes, one might expect that the cat would be similarly favoured. But no. This may well have something to do with the fact that your average pussy cat is so bally aloof. He reckons he's above all this corny joke nonsense.

As it is, the dogs almost sweep the board in this selection. And we begin with three classic crackers.

❦ *'I say, I say! Our dog doesn't eat meat.'*
'Your dog doesn't eat meat? Why not?'
'We don't give him any.'
—Oi!

❦ *'I say, I say! My dog's got no nose.'*
'How does he smell?'
'Awful.'

❦ *' I say, I say! I've just had my dog put down.'*
'Was he mad?'
'He was furious!'

Hiker spots a shepherd sitting in a field playing chess with his sheepdog. After watching the dog make several clever moves, the hiker remarks:

🎵 'I say! What a wonderful dog you have there!'
'He ain't so clever, friend. He's lost the last three games.'

🎵 *'I say, there's a black cat in the dining room.'*
'Don't worry—they're lucky.'
'This one certainly is. It's eating your dinner.'

Coalman arrives, and is given his instructions by a parrot:

🎵 'Half a ton, please.'
When he has finished the delivery, the coalman comments:
'You're a good talker, Polly.'
'Yes, and I can count, too. Bring the other bag.'

Customer at the pet shop:
🎵 *'Have you any dogs going cheap?'*
'Sorry, madam. All our dogs go "Woof".'

🎵 'I say, I say! My dog chases everyone he sees on a bike. What should I do?'
'Take the bike away from him immediately.'

🎵 *'Did you put the cat out?'*
'I didn't know it was on fire.'

🎵 'I say, why has your dog got those little brown boots on?'
'Because his little black ones are at the cobbler's.'

🎵 *Why is a pet shop a good place to visit if you haven't too much cash to spare?—Because not only will you find budgies going cheep, but many of them will be on higher perches.*

🎵 'I say, what kind of dog is that?'
'A Boxer.'
'Can't be a very good one—look at his face!'

99

How do you stop a dog barking in the back of a car?—Put him in the front.

 'I say, every day when I pass your house on my way to work, your dog bids me "Good Morning".'
'Impossible, old chap—he can't talk. It's that dog next door —he's a ventriloquist.'

 'I say, I say! I hear your dog enjoys a game of poker.'
'True—but he's not very good at it.'
'How's that?'
'Every time he gets a decent hand, he wags his tail.'

 'I say, I say! My dog can say its name.'
'Well, what's its name?'
'Woof.'

'I say—our dog bit my leg last night.'
'Did you put anything on it?'
'No. He liked it just as it was.'
—Oi!

TALKING POLITICS

Of all the best things in life which remain free, talking is perhaps the most fascinating. It seems to me quite, quite wonderful that you can—without any apparent pause for thought—rattle off a barrage of noise which will be instantly understood by anyone at whom you direct it.

As a rule, talking is definitely a Good Thing—even (though you may jib at this) when it is the politicians who are doing the talking.

Within limits, we should be allowed to say what we like to

whom we like. And they should be allowed to say what they like to us. For verbal combat is preferable to fisticuffs. As Churchill might have said: 'Jaw-jaw is better than broken-jaw.' Speech is a grand gift and I'm a great believer in making the most of it. Indeed, an accusation frequently levelled against me is that I never stop talking. Which is rubbish.

I have hours of dream-packed sleep each night during which no word passes my lips. And I also stop talking when I am alone. I may let loose a word or two on stubbing a toe on the bed leg, or shutting a finger in the car door—but these words do not really count, as they are howled rather than talked.

(By the way, if you are one of those people who mutter away to yourself occasionally, you may perhaps have wondered if you are going round the bend. For you will be well aware of the popular supposition that it is the 'First sign of madness, old boy!' You will be relieved to hear that I have it on excellent authority—a prof. who has studied speech and communication for more than thirty-five years—that this is not the case. He says there is nothing to worry about—and he catches himself at it once in a while. So if you're on your own and fancy a chat—feel free.)

There are some folk, however, for whom happiness is a Trappist Monastery. They get particularly steamed up about abusive jaw-jaw—the sort in which our politicians revel.

The Duke of Norfolk acted as spokesman for the Trappists when he said that he disliked intensely the 'petty squabbling. verbal sniping and muck-raking', and that he was sure the 'ordinary fellow in the street' was fed up with it.

Not this ordinary fellow! I regard the political petty squabbling and verbal sniping as great entertainment. I'm there on the touchline shouting for more—and pitching in my two-penn'orth.

In fact, today's politicians are a very mealy-mouthed shower in comparison with their predecessors. Listen to Disraeli's choice observation to Lord Palmerston: 'Your Lordship is like a favourite footman on easy terms with his mistress.'

Disraeli (Sock it to 'em, Dizzy!) was more forceful in his denunciation of the Irish political leader Daniel O'Connell—'a traitor with a bloody hand'. O'Connell retaliated by calling Disraeli a liar, said he was 'the most degraded of his species' and warned his audience against 'a miscreant of his abominable, foul and atrocious nature'.

Marvellous stuff, that.

And this is how O'Connell pictured members of the House of Lords: 'They are the soaped pigs of Society, the real swinish multitude. As obstinate and as ignorant and as brutish as their prototypes.'

Political abuse in the twentieth century has been less violent, but nonetheless entertaining.

Lloyd George described Neville Chamberlain as 'an adequate Lord Mayor of Birmingham in a lean year'. And he remarked that Sir John Simon had 'sat so long on the fence that the iron has entered his soul'.

Churchill dubbed Ramsay Mac 'the boneless wonder' and Attlee 'a sheep in sheep's clothing'. Bevan described the Tories as 'vermin' and his colleague Hugh Gaitskell as 'a desiccated calculating machine'.

Some years ago, Sir Alec Douglas-Home called the Socialists 'croaking crows', while Jim Callaghan called Sir Alec 'the Artful Dodger' in return.

And, keeping the sniping within the party, Lord Hailsham once said that if he had sat down for cards with a man who had spoken like Lord Salisbury 'I would leave the table before I lost too much money'.

Splendid, splendid!

My own favourite classic of verbal sniping in the Commons is that of an M.P. who said of another member: 'He has not the manners of a pig.' Duly rebuked by the Speaker, the M.P. replied: 'I beg to withdraw and apologize. The Hon. Member *has* the manners of a pig.'

Even the ladies have been quite catty on occasion. Dame Irene Ward said to Lady (then Dr Edith) Summerskill: 'Oh, Edith! You really are an ass.' And the doctor said of the dame: 'I am surprised that she should be so feline.'

We need not go into the verbal sniping that has enlivened more recent parliamentary proceedings. This is fresh in our minds. But to those who share the misgivings of His Grace the Duke of Norfolk, I would cite an exchange many years ago in the House of Lords. An aged peer, in the course of delivering an extremely dreary speech, droned: 'And now, my Lords, I ask myself this question . . .'

A voice interrupted: 'And a damned dull answer you'll get.'

Yes. And without the verbal sniping, a damned dull bunch of politicians *we'd* get.

I say ❦ encore!

(A Climactic Gallimaufry of quick-fire quips and cross-talk)

Ladies and gentlemen. Before the curtain call, I have been asked to make one or two announcements.

You are requested to remain in your seats until the conclusion of the performance, and then to leave in an orderly fashion. Your attention is drawn to collecting boxes placed conveniently at either side of the exit. A fish and chip supper, with Mrs Armstrong's home-made trifle to follow, will be served in the Ebenezer Hall Annexe immediately after these proceedings. I thank you for your kind attention, and—in anticipation—for your generous applause.

Right-ho, chaps—let it rip!

❦ *'I say, I say—I used to be a tap-dancer. But I had to give it up.'*
'Give up tap-dancing—why?'
'Kept falling in the sink.'
—Oi!

❦ 'Strange pair of shoes you're wearing—one black and one brown. Must be unique.'
'Not at all. I've another pair like these at home.'

Two hungry cowboys lost in the desert.
❦ *'Food at last,' one shouts. 'There's a bacon tree on top of that ridge.'*
He gallops off, but is back in a trice with his hat shot through with arrows. 'That was no bacon tree. It was an 'ambush.'

'I say, I say! Can you play the violin?'
'Don't know. I've never tried.'

Out for his morning constitutional, the Bishop sees a little girl trying to reach the knocker of a door.
 'Allow me, my dear,' says the Bishop. And gives the knocker a sharp rat-a-tat-tat.
'That's it,' says the little girl. 'Now run like hell.'

 'I say, I say! I've just seen a chap removing my front gate.'
'Why didn't you stop him?'
'Didn't like to. I thought he might take offence.'

 'I say, I say! My neighbour's dog barks all night and I can't sleep. What should I do?'
'Buy the dog from him—then he won't be able to sleep.'

 'I say—I've discovered a marvellous slimming diet.'
'What's that?'
'Eat plenty of dripping.'
'Why dripping?'
'Constant dripping wears away a stone.'

A reporter visits a prisoner in his cell.
 'Good morning. I'd just like to take a few notes.'
'You be careful, guv'nor. That's what I'm in here for.'

New prisoner arrives in the cell.
 'What are you in for?'
'Careless driving. Forgot I didn't own the car.'

 Dustman: 'Where's yer bin, missus?'
'We've been to Blackpool for a fortnight.'

Postman knocks.
 'I say, is this parcel for you? The name's obliterated.'
' 'Fraid not. My name's Harrison.'

'What do you call a window cleaner wearing nine balaclava helmets?'
'Anything you like. He won't hear you anyway.'

'I say, I weighed only six ounces when I was born.'
'Gracious. Did you live?'
'I certainly did. You should see me now.'

Orderly officer to recruit:
'Any complaints?'
'Yes, sir—this stew's funny.'
'Then why ain't you laughing, lad?'

Naval captain signals Base Hospital:
'Have case of Beri-Beri aboard. What action shall I take?'
'Give it to the Marines, they'll drink anything.'

'I say, I say! A crab's just bitten my toe.'
'Which one?'
'Don't know. All crabs look alike to me.'

Two cannibals chatting over lunch:
'I don't like the look of my wife.'
'Leave her then. Just eat the potatoes.'

Missionary to native chief: 'Me come in great silver bird.'
Chief: 'Really, old chap? I always go by 'plane.'

'How much is that corset?'
'£3, including tax.'
'Anything cheaper with elastic?'

'I say, I say! How do you get down from an elephant?'
'I don't know. How do you get down from an elephant?'
'You don't. You get it from a swan.'

107

And finally some variations on traditional themes with which you will be only too familiar:

❧ 'I say, I say! Who was that lady I seen you with last night?'
'You mean "I saw".'
'Sorry—who was that eyesore I seen you with last night?'

Magician to girl assistant:
❧ *'Who was that lady I sawed you with last night?'*
'That was no lady—that was my half-sister.'

❧ 'Why did the chicken cross the road?'
'Because it was a fowl proceeding.'

❧ *'Why did the unwashed chicken cross the road twice?'*
'Because it was a dirty double-crosser.'

❧ 'Why did the chicken cross the road?'
'To get his old age pension.'

—You don't get it? Well, neither did the chicken—he wasn't sixty-five.

OI!